懷玉被褐聖人

宗演書

太上老君

篇 應 感 上 太

Treatise on Response
& Retribution

Lao Tze

Translated from the Chinese by

D. T. Suzuki & Paul Carus

Containing Introduction, Chinese Text, Verbatim Translation,
Translation, Explanatory Notes and Moral Tales

Edited by

Paul Carus

With Sixteen Plates by Chinese Artists and a
Frontispiece by Keichyu Yamada

1973

THE OPEN COURT PUBLISHING COMPANY
LaSalle, Illinois

Printed in the United States of America

ISBN: 0–87548–244–9

The Library of Congress catalogued the original printing
of this title as follows:

T'ai-shang kan-ying p'ien.
. . . .T'ai-shang kan-ying p'ien; treatise of the Exalted one
on response and retribution; translated from the Chinese by
Teitaro Suzuki and Dr. Paul Carus; containing introduction, Chinese text, verbatim translation, translation, explanatory notes and moral tales, edited by Dr. Paul Carus. With
sixteen plates by Chinese artists and a frontispiece by Keichyu Yamada. Chicago, Ill., The Open Court Publishing
Co.; London, K. Paul, Trench, Trubner & Co., Ltd. 1926

  3 p l., (3)–139 p front., illus., plates. 21 cm

  1. Taoism. 1. Suzuki, Daisetz Teitaro, 1870– tr. II. Carus
Paul, 1852–1919, ed. and tr.

BL1900.T3S8

                                          6–28775
Library of Congress   (63h1/2)   Provisional

CONTENTS.

五福

壽　富　康寧

攸好德　考終命

INTRODUCTION

INTRODUCTION.

IF the popularity of books must be measured by either the number of copies in which they appear or the devotion of their readers, the *T'ai-Shang Kan-Ying P'ien,* i. e., "The Treatise of the Exalted One on Response and Retribution," will probably have to be assigned the first place of all publications on the globe. Its editions exceed even those of the Bible and Shakespeare, which of all the books published in the Western world are most numerous, and many millions of devout Chinese believe that great merit is gained by the dissemination of the book.

The *T'ai-Shang Kan-Ying P'ien* is a work of Taoist piety and ethics. It is not so deep as Lao Tze's *Tao-Teh-King,* but its moral maxims which are noble and pure, are presented with a more popular directness.

The main idea of the title is expressed in the words *Kan,* "response," and *Ying,* "retribution," which mean that in the spiritual realm of heaven there is "a response" to our sentiments, finding expression in "a retribution" of our deeds.

T'ai-Shang, literally, "the Grandly High" or "the Exalted One," is a current name of Lao Tze, the old philosopher, author of the *Tao-Teh-King,* who is revered by Taoists as the great teacher of mankind, the superior man, and the highest authority of religious truth.

Lao Tze's philosophy has percolated into the Chinese nation and we can distinguish three strata: the first represented by the *Tao-Teh-King,* the second by the *T'ai-Shang Kan-Ying P'ien,* and the third by the stories appended to it. The first is profound though partly obscure, the second elevating, yet mixed with those popular notions which belong to the domain of mythology, and the third is devout in tone, but sometimes silly in its details.

The text of the *T'ai-Shang Kan-Ying P'ien* consists of several parts: (1) an introduction, (2) moral injunctions, (3) a description of evil-doers and their penalty, (4) sayings from various sources, and (5) the conclusion. Internal evidence suggests that we have before us a compilation in which we can distinguish at least three authors of decidedly different characters. The introduction (being itself a compilation) and the passage "Punishment of Evil-Doers" apparently come from the pen of the final redactor, presumably a *Tao Shih,* a Taoist scholar or priest, while the second part, "Moral Injunctions," constitutes the most valuable portion of the book. The third part, "The Description of Evil-Doers," is written by a moralizer, or even denouncer, rather than a moralist. Possibly (nay even probably) he is identical with the final redactor, but scarcely with the author of the "Moral Injunctions." He has incorporated quotations from an unknown Taoist source (e. g., the beautiful passage, 1170-1198) and lines from the Buddhist *Dhammapada* (1210 ff.).

The passage on good words, good thoughts, and good deeds, and also on evil words, evil thoughts, and evil deeds sound like remote but clear echoes of the Zendavesta.

The second part, "Moral Injunctions," reaches the loftiest height of a truly moral and catholic spirit. It is short enough, but with all its conciseness every word of it is noble and deserves a place side by side with the best religious literature of the world. It should be quoted and requoted, learned by heart and acted upon by all mankind. The third part, "A Description of Evil-Doers," is on a lower level. The moral spirit of its author is narrower, more sectarian, nor free from superstitious notions. The introduction of the treatise (1-147) exhibits the attitude of a disciple,—a faithful devotee, who, however, has merely touched the hem of the Master's garment.

Some passages of the introduction, and perhaps its final redaction, seem to be written by the author of the third part.

The treatise, which is decidedly a work of Taoist devotion, shows obvious influences of Buddhist and Confucian* doctrines. Though it is not a canonical book its authoritative character is universally recognized in China, and it may be regarded as a typical exposition of the moral convictions of the average Chinese. It has become the most important guide of the people's conscience.

Though the *T'ai-Shang Kan-Ying P'ien* may not have existed in its present shape before the fifteenth or sixteenth century, it contains passages which are very old, and though we are not prepared to give a detailed analysis of its contents, we will state here that some portions are quite ancient, belonging to the sixth century B. C. This is true not only of the Con-

* Especially 172-175.

fucian and Buddhist maxims but also of the first sentence. Rev. James Legge makes the following statement concerning the words, 4 ff., in one of the footnotes of his translation: "This paragraph, after the three first characters, is found in *Zo Khwan* under the tenth and eleventh notices in the twenty-third year of Duke Hsiang (549 B. C.),—part of an address to a young nobleman by the officer of Min *Zze-mâ*."

The mythological background of the arguments of the *T'ai-Shang Kan-Ying P'ien* can be characterized as superstitious by those only who know nothing of comparative religion and are not familiar with the fact that the idea of Recording Angels is all but universal in a certain phase of the history of religion.

The treatise has its shortcomings, both in form and contents. Its materials are not systematically arranged, and side by side with maxims of highest morality we find such trivial injunctions as the one that we should not cook food with rotten sticks. Further, the idea of retribution is upon the whole conceived to work in a mechanical and external way, being doled out in exact proportions of merit and demerit. Yet, after all, if we consider the significance of its main idea, who will deny that there is a retribution which, though not meted out with a tape measure, is after all unfailing? We will judge mildly, if we consider that even in the Lord's Prayer God is asked to "forgive us our debts as we forgive our debtors" —a passage which sounds more mercantile in the original which means "Let off to us our debts as also we let off our debtors." The suggestion is made here as well as in our Chinese treatise, that as our dealings are, so Heaven and God will deal with us; and considering all in all, the underlying idea is true.

There is another weak point in the religious notions of our treatise, viz., the belief in demons which in the stories involves the superstition of obsession. But let us remember that the New Testament is full of it, and the era of witch persecution in Europe which is the worst aspect of obsession, is about simultaneous with the date of the *T'ai-Shang Kan-Ying P'ien*.

The Chinese may not as yet have passed entirely the stage of childhood diseases, but let us remember that the European race too had its measles.

Without being blind to the shortcomings of our "Treatise on Response and Retribution," considered as a whole, we cannot deny that its general tendency is noble, and true,—and, we may add, also practical.

Practical it is, and "practical" means that it is as exactly adapted to the life and views of the people of its origin as if it had been prepared for them and dictated to its author by Divine Providence. From this point of view we may say that it is a work of prophetic inspiration.

The shortcomings of the *T'ai-Shang Kan-Ying P'ien* appear to greater disadvantage in the stories which are appended to its moral maxims. Here the doctrine of the Exalted One reaches the broad strata of the masses, but even in this form a presentation of religious notions is needed so as to render its moral maxims intelligible among the superstitious. Perhaps we should say *vice versa*, that we see here how the uneducated assimilate a religious doctrine to their special wants. Every one has the religion he deserves, because every one adapts himself to his own spiritual needs.

The first translation of the *T'ai-Shang Kan-Ying*

P'ien, made by a Western scholar, is Stanislas Julien's
Le livre des recompenses et des peines, printed at
Paris for the Oriental Translation Fund of Great
Britain and Ireland. It contains the Chinese text of
the book and in addition to the French translation
of the main text, a French translation of the glosses
and stories of the Chinese commentator, which swell
the work to a volume of considerable size. The English version of Prof. Robert K. Douglas is a translation of extracts from this French edition made by
M. Julien. It appeared in his excellent little volume
Confucianism and Taouism, (pp. 256-271) in the series
of *Non-Christian Religious Systems,* published by the
Society for promoting Christian Knowledge, London,
1839. Finally Prof. James Legge has translated our
treatise in the *Sacred Books of the East,* Vol. XL,
pp. 233-246, under the title *T'ai Shang, Tractate of
Actions and their Retributions.*

* * *

Our text and illustrations of the stories are fac-
simile reproductions taken (with the exception of
one picture) from a collection of Chinese texts made
in Japan by Chinese scribes and artists. The scribe
calls himself Lai Ho Nien of Kwei Ping. Stanislas
Julien's text agrees pretty closely with ours—closely
enough to render any further comments redundant.
The stories appended to the main body of the book
seem to differ considerably in different editions. At
any rate they vary greatly in the French and Japanese
versions at our disposal. They are of inferior worth
and we deem it sufficient to have them here represented
in extracts.

The present translation of the *T'ai-Shang Kan-
Ying P'ien* is a product of the common labors of Mr.

Teitaro Suzuki and the Editor. Mr. Suzuki, who among the scholars of Eastern Asia living in our midst is one of the best authorities on the religious texts of ancient China, has gathered the necessary information concerning the lexicographical, grammatical, and archæological meaning of the text; while the Editor is responsible for the arrangement of the whole, together with the final version of the English text in both the verbatim translation which is intended to be lexicographically exact, and the translation proper which is meant to offer a readable English version.

* * *

Our frontispiece is a picture of the great philosopher Lao Tze whom the Taoists call *T'ai Shang,* The Most Exalted One; or more fully *T'ai Shang Lao Chün,* i. e., The Most Exalted Ancient Master. The artist represents him with a little square cap usually worn by the common people and dressed, not in silk, but in rough woolen garments; for we know that he practised the simplicity which he preached. But, in contrast to this simple exterior, his countenance indicates a rare depth of thought and his eyes beam with benevolence. We have set above the picture a quotation from his great book, the *Tao-Teh-King* (Chapter 70) which reads:

Shang jan pei hö, hwai yü.
"A saint wears wool, but in his bosom are jewels."

In addition to the illustrations which are inserted in the stories to which they belong, the present edition of the *Kan-Ying P'ien* is adorned by a few apposite sketches and ornamental designs. Facing page 1, the fly leaf of the Introduction, we have the Chinese

characters which denote the five blessings. These are,
(1) longevity, (2) riches, (3) peacefulness and serenity, (4) love of virtue, and (5) [at an advanced] age
a [happy] consummation of life.

The gate of honor which appears on page 48, bears
an inscription which reads: "The Tao (i. e., divine
reason) penetrates the past and the present"; in other
words, it is eternal.

The inscription of the gate represented on page 80
reads: "Virtue harmonizes heaven and earth."

The design on the book cover bears the conven-
tionalized form of the longevity symbol so popular
among the Chinese.

*   *   *

The numbers of the words in the Chinese text
(twelve hundred and seventy-seven characters in all
not counting the heading nor the scribe's signature)
are written underneath each column of both the Chinese text and the verbatim translation, and follow
also the corresponding paragraphs of the English
version.

Each footnote figure following the word to which
it refers, is inserted in both the verbatim translation
and the English text.

In those places where a word-for-word translation of the text would demand another order in English than obtains in the original Chinese, we have num-
bered the words as they would read in English.

The italicized headings of the several parts are
placed within parentheses, because they are not in the
original text and have been made by the Editor of the
English version solely for the convenience of English
readers.

篇 應 感 上 太

CHINESE TEXT WITH VERBATIM
TRANSLATION

太上感應篇

太上感應篇

太上曰禍福無門惟人自召善
惡之報如影隨形是以天地有
司過之神依人所犯輕重以奪
人算算減則貧耗多逢憂患人
皆惡之刑禍隨之吉慶避之惡

The Grandly	The Grandly	(and) evil	recording	man's	all[10]
High One's[1]	High One	's[5]	crimes	term of life.	hate
Response[2]	says:[3]	reward	's[5]	Term of life	him;
(and) Re-tribution[2]	Curses	is like	spirits.	(being) reduced	punish-ments
Treatise.	(and) blessings	shadow	(1) Pro-portion-ately to[7]	then	(and) curses
	have no	following	(5) men	(he be-comes) poor	follow
	gates,[4]	object.	(4) of that in which	(and) des-titute.[9]	him;
	but	There-	(6) trans-gress	Many times	good
	man	fore[6]	(2) light-ness	he meets with	luck
	himself	heaven	(3) (or) gravity,	calamity	shuns
	invites (them).	(and) earth	thereby[8]	(and) trouble.[9]	him;
	Good	have	is cut off	Men	evil

太上感應篇

星災之。算盡則死。又有三台北
斗神君在人頭上。錄人罪惡。奪
其紀算。又有三尸神在人身中。
每到庚申日。輒上詣天曹。言人
罪過。月晦之日竈神亦然。凡人
有過。大則奪紀。小則奪算。其過

stars	(5) con-stella-tion[12]	of them	When-ever	crimes	having
pursue	(2) spirit-	12 years	arrives	(and) offences.	offences,
him.	lords;	(or) 100 days.	Kêng	(On the) month's	the great ones
Term of life	they are	Further,	Shên[14]	ultimo[16]	then
(being) exhausted	(2) men's	there are	day,	's	deprive
then	(3) heads	the three	then	day	(them of) 12 years;
(he) dies.	(1) above.	body-	they ascend	the hearth-	the small ones
Further,	(They) record	spirits[13]	reaching	spirit[16]	then
there are	men's	existing	heavenly	also	deprive (them of)
the three	crimes	(2) man's	master[15]	(does) the same.	100 days.
(1) coun-cilors'[11]	(and) sins,[9]	(3) person	(and) tell of	Of all	These
(4) (of the) Northern	cutting off	(1) within.	men's	men	offences
61-72	73-84	85-96	97-108	109-120	121-132

太上感應篇

大小有數百事。欲求長生者先。
須避之。是道則進。非道則退。不
履邪徑。不欺暗室。積德累功。慈
心於物。忠孝友悌。正己化人。矜
孤恤寡。敬老懷幼。昆蟲草木。猶
不可傷。宜憫人之凶。樂人之善。

great	ought to	tread on	heart	orphans	not
(and) small	shun	evil	(turn) toward	(and) assist	are to be
are	them.[18]	path.	creatures.	widows.	injured.
several	The right	Not	Be faithful,	Respect	You should
hundred	way	be false to yourself[20]	filial,	the old	feel grieved at
affairs.	then	(in) dark	friendly,	(and) be kind to	men
Anxious	advances;[19]	room.[21]	brotherly.[22]	children.	's[5]
to seek	the wrong	Accumulate	Having rectified	The many (various)	misfortunes,
long	way	virtue,	self	insects,	rejoice at
life[17]	then	increase	(then) convert	herbs	men
the ones	leads backwards[19].	merits.	men.	(and) trees	's[5]
first	Not	(With) a compassionate	Pity	even	goodness.

篇應感上太

濟人之急。救人之危。見人之得。
如己之得。見人之失。如己之失。
不彰人短。不炫己長。遏惡揚善。
推多取少。受辱不怨。受寵若驚。
施恩不求報。與人不追悔。所謂
善人。人皆敬之。天道祐之。福祿

Help	as	Not	Renounce	Extend	are good
men	self	make mani-fest	much,	help,	men.
's[5]	's[5]	men's	accept	not	Men
indigence.	gain.	shortcom-ings.	little.	seeking	all[10]
Rescue	Regard	Not	Suffer	reward.	honor
men	men	display	humilia-tion	Give to	them.
(in) their[5]	's[5]	own	not	men	Heavenly
danger.	loss.	excel-lence.	bearing grudge.	not	reason's[24]
Regard	as	Stay	Receive	after-wards	grace
men	self	evil,	favor	regret-ting.	(is upon) them.[25]
's[5]	's[5]	promote	as if	Those who	Bliss
gain	loss.	goodness.	sur-prised.[23]	are thus	(and) abund-ance[9]

太上感應篇

隨之。眾邪遠之。神靈衛之。所作
必成。神仙可冀。欲求天仙者。當
立一千三百善。欲求地仙者。當
立三百善。苟或非義而動。背理
而行。以惡為能。忍作殘害。陰賊
良善。暗侮君親。慢其先生。叛其

follow	surely	do	do	even	the good
them.	succeeds.	one	three	they walk.	(and) law-abiding.[9]
All	(To become) spiritual	thousand	hundred	In	In dark
evils[26]	saints	three	(acts of) goodness.	evil	they despise
keep away	they can	hundred	If[28]	they take	superiors
(from) them.[5]	aspire for.	(acts of) goodness.	some	delight.[30]	(and) parents.
Angel-	Those anxious	Those anxious	not	Brutally	They disregard
spirits	to seek	to seek	righteously	they inflict	their
guard	(to be) heavenly	(to be) earthly	even	harm	earlier
them.	saints[27]	saints	behave,	(and) damage.[9]	born.
That which	the ones,	the ones,	against	insidiously	They rebel against
they undertake	should	should	reason[29]	they injure	their
277-288	289-300	301-312	313-324	325-336	337-348

太上感應篇

所事詆諸無識。謗諸同學虛誣

詐偽。攻訐宗親。剛強不仁。狠戾

自用。是非不當。向背乖宜。虐下

取功。諂上希旨。受恩不感。念怨

不休。輕蔑天民。擾亂國政。賞及

非義。刑及無辜。殺人取財。傾人

those whom	deceive	(and) self-	they appropriate	not	(the) un-
they serve.	(and) play the hypocrite.[9]	willed.	merits.	they keep quiet.	righteous.
They deceive	They attack[31]	Right	By cringing	In levity	Punishment
those	(and) expose	(and) wrong	to superiors	they make light of[9]	they extend to
not having	kith	not	they curry	heaven's	(the) in-
information.	(and) kin.[9]	they match.	favor.	people.[33]	offensive.
They slander	They are stubborn,	Avowals	Received	They agitate	They kill
those	obstinate[9]	(and) disavowals	favors	and disturb[9]	men
of the same	(and) not	(are) against	not	the empire's	to take
study.	humane;	the ought.[32]	they feel.	order.	their property.
They lie,	cruel,	By oppressing	Remembering	Prizes	They oust
calumniate,	irrational,	subordinates	hatred	they extend to	men

太上感應篇

取位誅降戮服貶正排賢淩孤
逼寡棄法受賂以直為曲以曲
為直入輕為重見殺加怒知過
不改知善不為自罪引他壅塞
方術訕謗聖賢侵淩道德射飛
逐走發蟄驚棲填穴覆巢傷胎

to seize	they wrong	they take	not	the divination	they chase
their positions.	widows.	straight.	(they) correct (them.)	craft.[35]	the running;
They slay	They disregard	They put down	They know	They vilify	they expose
those who surrender	law	light	the good	(and) disparage[9]	the hidden;
(and) slaughter	to receive	as	(but) not	the holy	they surprise
the submissive.	bribes.	heavy.	(they) do (it.)	(and) the wise.	the nestling;
They malign	For	Witnessing	(Into) own	They deride	they close up
the just;	straight	execution,	crime	(and) ridicule[9]	holes;
they expel	they take	they add	they draw	reason	they upset
the wise;	crooked.	harshness.	others.[34]	(and) virtue.[36]	nests;
they molest	For	Knowing	They obstruct	They shoot	they injure
orphans;	crooked	their faults	(and) thwart[9]	the flying;	the foetus;
421-432	433-444	445-456	457-468	469-480	481-492

太上感應篇

破卵、願人有失、毀人成功、危人自安、減人自益、以惡易好、以私廢公、竊人之能、蔽人之善、形人之醜、訏人之私、耗人貨財、離人骨肉、侵人所愛、助人為非、逞志作威、辱人求勝、敗人苗稼、破人

they break	self	they neglect	's[5]	bone	they make for
the egg.	to save.	the public.	foibles.	(and) flesh.[37]	power.
They wish	They impoverish	They steal	They expose	(1) They attack[7]	They degrade
men	men,	others	others	(4) others	others
to have	self	's[5]	's[5]	(2) that which	to seek
loss.	to profit.	excellence.	secrets.	(3) is dear to.	success.
They disparage	With	They hide	They waste	They assist	They destroy
men's	worthless	others	others'	others	others'
achievement	they exchange	's[5]	goods	in doing	young plants
(of) merit.	valuables.	good.	(and) property.[9]	wrong.	(and) farming.[9]
They endanger	For	They manifest	They separate	With unbridled	They break up
men,	the private	others	others'	desire	others'

太上感應篇

婚姻。苟富而驕。苟免無恥。認恩
推過。嫁禍賣惡。沽買虛譽。包貯
險心。挫人所長護己所短乘威
迫脅。縱暴殺傷、無故剪裁非禮
烹宰。散棄五穀勞擾眾生、破人
之家取其財寶。決水放火以害

(relation between) bride-groom	(and) dis-claim	treach-erous	they threaten	they roast	's[5]
(and) bride.	faults.	heart.	(and) intimi-date.[9]	cattle.[41]	houses,
Improp-erly	They give in marriage	They crush	With unre-strained	They scatter	to take
(they have grown) rich;	evils;[39]	in others	barbarism	(and) waste[9]	their
in addi-tion	they sell	that which	they kill	the five	property
they are vulgar.	wrongs.	is excel-lent.	and stab.	cereals.[42]	(and) valu-ables.[9]
Improp-erly	They sell	They guard	Without	They trouble	They mis-direct
they have es-caped,[38]	(and) buy	in self	reason	(and) annoy[9]	water,
(yet) have no	vain-	that which is	they cut	many	(and) set
shame.	glory.	short.	(and) clip[40] (cloth).	people.	fire,
They rec-ognise	They conceal	Riding on	Not	They break into	thereby
favors	(and) keep	power	cere-monial	others	to destroy

篇應感上太

民居衆亂規模以敗人功損人
器物以窮人用、見他榮貴願他
流貶、見他富有願他破散見他
色美起心私之負他貨財願他
身死干求不遂便生咒恨見他
失便便說他過見他體相不具

people's	utensils	run down	features	person	lose
resi-dences.	(and) things	(and) fail.[9]	beautiful,	to die.	(their) vantage,
They disturb	thereby	Seeing	they are roused	(When their) requests	then
(and) disar-range[9]	inter-fering with	others	in heart	(and) de-mands[9]	they gossip
regula-tions	men's	wealth-	to seduce	not	(of) others'
(and) plans,[9]	conve-niences.	having,	them.	are acceded to,	failures.
thereby	When seeing	they desire	When owing	then	Seeing
ruining	others	others	to others	they pro-duce (lit. "grow")	others'
men's	succeed	to be bank-rupt	goods	curses	bodily
success.	(and) prosper,[9]	(and) scatter.[9]	(and) prop-erty,	(and) hatred.[9]	features
They spoil	they wish	When seeing	they wish	Seeing	not
men's	others	others'	others'	others	perfect,

太上感應篇

而笑之。見他才能可稱而抑之。

埋蠱厭人。用藥殺樹。恚怒師傅。

抵觸父兄。強取強求。好侵好奪。

擄掠至富。巧詐求遷。賞罰不平。

逸樂過節。苛虐其下。恐嚇於他。

怨天尤人。呵風罵雨。鬬合爭訟。

even	They bury	They resist	(They make) raids	They seek	They accuse
they deride	vermin[43]	and provoke[9]	(and) depredations[9]	(and) take pleasure	heaven
them.	to control	father	to get	beyond	(and) find fault with
Seeing	others.[44]	(and) elders.	rich.	measure.	men.
others'	They employ	With violence	By artful	They harass	They blame
talent	drugs	they seize,	tricks	(and) tyrannise[9]	the wind;
(and) ability[9]	to kill	with violence	they seek	their	they rail at
to be	trees.	they demand.	promotion.	subordinates.	the rain.
praiseworthy,	(They are) ill-humored	They delight in	They reward	They terrify	They stir
even	(and) angry to[9]	fraud,	(and) punish	(and) threaten	party
they suppress	teachers	they delight in	not	to overawe	strife
it (the fact.)	(and) instructors.[9]	robbery.	evenly.	others.	(and) lawsuits.

篇應感上太

妄逐朋黨。用妻妾語。違父母訓。

得新忘故。口是心非。貪冒於財。

欺罔其上。造作惡語。讒毀平人。

毀人稱直。罵神稱正棄順效逆。

背親向疏。指天地以證鄙懷。引

神明而鑑猥事。施與後悔。假借

Without cause	They acquire	they deceive	They slander	They turn back on	spirits
they follow	the new;	(and) cheat[9]	men	the near,	bright,
factious	they forget	their	(and) claim to be	(and) seek	even
associations.[45]	the old.	superiors.	straight.	the distant.[46]	to witness
They rely on	Their mouth	They manufacture	They mock	They point	(their) degrading
wife's	asserts,	(and) make[9]	spirits	at heaven	deeds.
(and) maids'	(what their) heart	vile	(and) claim	(and) earth[47]	Charity
gossip.	denies.	talks.	to be right.	thereby	they give,
They disobey	Greedy	They traduce	They cast aside	to witness	afterwards
father's	(and) shameless[9]	(and) slander	good cause,	their mean	they regret.
(and) mother's	for	innocent	(and) follow	thoughts.	They borrow
instruction.	wealth,	men.	wrong cause.	They draw	(and) accept loans[9]

太上感應篇

不還分外營求。力上施設。淫慾過度。心毒貌慈穢食餧人。左道惑眾。短尺狹度。輕秤小升。以偽雜真。採取姦利。壓良為賤。謾驀愚人。貪婪無厭。咒詛求直。嗜酒悖亂。骨月念爭。男不忠良。女不

not	exceed	they mislead	they mix	simple-minded	they become rebellious
to return [them.]	(all) measure.	people.	the genuine.	men.	(and) unruly.⁹
Their lot	Their heart	They shorten	They take	They are greedy	(With) bone
exceeding	is venomous,	the foot,	(and) seize⁹	(and) covetous⁹	(and) flesh³⁷
they scheme	their face	they narrow	illegitimate	without	(they are) angry
(and) demand⁹	compassionate.	the measure.	profit.⁴⁸	satiety.	(and) quarrelsome.⁹
Their means	With filthy	They lighten	They compel	They curse	As husbands⁴⁹
above,	food	the scales,	respectable (people)	(and) swear⁹	not
they contrive	they feed	they reduce	to become	to seek	they are faithful
(and) plan.⁹	men.	the peck.	lowly.	vindication.	(and) kind.
Their lusty	With left-handed (heterodox)	With	They betray	When indulging	As wives⁴⁹
desires	religion (lit. *Tao*)	the false	(and) deceive	in liquor	not

太上感應篇

柔順。不和其室。不敬其夫。每好
矜誇。常行妒忌。無行於妻子。失
禮於舅姑。輕慢先靈。違逆上命。
作為無益。懷挾外心。自咒咒他。
偏憎偏愛。越井越竈。跳食跳人。
損子墮胎。行多隱僻。晦臘歌舞。

(they are) gentle	bragging	propriety	They make	They are partial	They kill
(and) obeying.	(and) conceit.	for	(and) do[9]	in) hatred,	the baby,
Not	Always	father-in-law	(the) not-	they are partial	they cause abortion of
in harmony	they practice	(and)ther mother-in-law.	useful.	(in) love.	the fœtus.
(with) their	jealousy	They make light of	They harbor	They step over	(4) They do deeds
rooms[50] (i. e., wives).	(and) suspicion.[9]	(and) slight[9]	and) keep[9]	the well.[53]	(1) many
Not	(They are) without	(their) ancestor's	a treacherous	They step over	(2) clandestine
they respect	manners	spirit.	heart.[51]	the hearth.	(3) (and) wrong.
their	to	They disobey	Self[52]	They jump over	The last day of the month
husbands.	wife	(and) are unmindful of[9]	they curse;	the food,	(and) the last day of the year
Always	(and) children.	their superiors'	they curse	they jump over	they sing
they delight in	They lack	orders.	men.	a person.	(and) dance.[54]

太上感應篇

朔旦號怒。對北涕唾及溺。對竈
吟詠及哭。又以竈火燒香穢柴
作食。夜起裸露。八節行刑。唾流
星。指虹霓。輒指三光久視日月。
春月燎獵。對北惡罵。無故殺龜
打蛇。如是等罪。司命隨其輕重。

First day of the month,	they sing	they prepare	stars,	In spring	they strike
first day of the year,	(and) hum	food.	they point	month	snakes.
they swear	and	At night	at rainbows'	(with) fire	For such as
angrily.	weep.	they rise	irridescence. [59]	they hunt. [61]	these
Facing	Further,	and nakedness	Hastily	Facing	several
the North[55]	with	they expose. [57]	they point at	North,	crimes
they snivel	the hearth	(On the) eight	the three	heinously	the controllers
(and) spit	fire	season-festivals[58]	luminaries. [60]	they scold.	of destiny,
and	they burn	they execute	Long	Without	according to
urinate.	incense. [56]	punishment.	they gaze at	cause	their
Facing	With filthy	They spit at	sun	they kill	lightness
the hearth[55]	faggots	falling	(and) moon.	tortoises;	(and) gravity,

997-1008   1009-1020   1021-1032   1033-1044   1045-1056   1057-1068

篇應感上太

奪其紀算。算盡則死。死有餘責。
乃殃及子孫。又諸橫取人財者。
乃計其妻子家口以當之漸至
死喪。若不死喪。則有水火盜賊。
遺亡器物疾病口舌諸事以當
妄取之直。又枉殺人者。是易刀

they deprive	then	then	death	losses	for un-lawful
people's	evil luck	are set off (for them)	in exculpation.	(and) bereavements[9]	seizure
12 years	is transferred	their	If	of goods	's[5]
(or) 100 days.	to children	wives	not	(and) effects, [9]	justice.
Lease of life	(and) grand children.	(and) children	at death	(by) disease	Further,
(being) ex hausted	Further,	(and) other family	exculpated,	(and) illness[9]	(2) who wrongfully
then	(1) all	members,	then	(by mouth (and) tongue / ill repute)	(3) kill
they die.	(3) wrongfully	thereby	they have		(4) men
(If) at death	(4) seize	to compensate	water,	(By) all (such)	(1) the ones,
there is	(5) others'	it	fire,	affairs,	they
left	(6) property,	by degrees	theft,	thereby	exchange[62]
offence (unexpiated)	(2) the ones who	reaching	robbery,	compensate	weapons

太上感應篇

兵而相殺也。取非義之財者譬
如漏脯救饑酖酒止渴。非不暫
飽。死亦及之。夫心起於善善雖
未為而吉神已隨之。或心起於
惡。惡雖未為而凶神已隨之。其
有曾行惡事後自改悔。諸惡莫

(and) arms,[9]	are like (those who)	satisfaction,	not yet	bad,	having
and	(with) dripping-water,[65](i.e. tainted)	death	done;	bad	before
mutually	meat	also	verily	though	practised
(each other) they kill,[65]	relieve	reaches	good	not yet	bad
indeed.	hunger,	them.	spirits	done,	deeds,
(Who) seize	(or with) poisoned	If	already	verily	hence-forth
in-	liquor	(a man's) heart	follow	evil	them-selves
justice	quench, (lit. "stop")	be awakened	him.	spirits	should mend
's[5]	thirst.	to	If	already	(and) repent.[64]
property	(Though they are) not	good,	(a man's) heart	follow	(If) all
the ones,	without	good	be awakened	him.	evils
to illustrate,	tempo-rary	though	to	Those	not

太上感應篇

作眾善奉行久久必獲吉慶所。

謂轉禍為福也故吉人語善視

善行善。一日有三善。三年天必

降之福凶人語惡視惡行惡一

日有三惡。三年天必降之禍胡

不勉而行之。　桂平賴鶴年敬書

they do,	to speak,	good,	(will) shower (on)	day	not
(if) all	they transform	practising	him	being possessed of	be diligent
good	curse	good.	bliss.	the three	and
they promote	(and) make	(Each) one	Unlucky	evils,	comply with
(and) do,[9]	bliss	day	(the) man	(within) three	this?
long	indeed.	having	speaking	years,	Kwei
(and) long,	Therefore,	the three	evil,	Heaven	Ping
surely	blessed	good[65] (things)	contemplating	surely	Lai-
they obtain	(the) man	(within) three	evil,	(will) shower (on)	'Ho
happiness	speaking	years,	practising	him	Nien (has)
(and) felicity	good,	Heaven	evil.	curses.	reverently
So	contemplating	surely	(Each) one	Why	written (this).

1213-1224   1225-1236   1237-1248   1249-1260   1261-1272   1273-1284

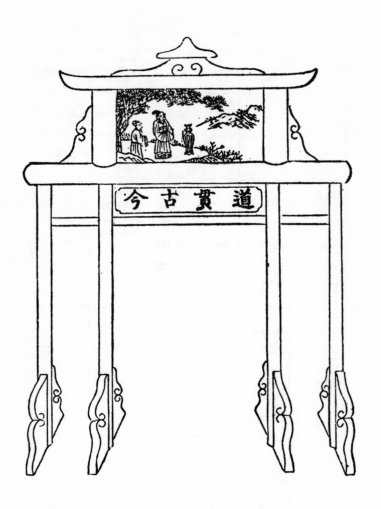

道貫古今

TREATISE OF THE EXALTED ONE ON RESPONSE AND RETRIBUTION

TREATISE OF THE EXALTED ONE[1] ON RESPONSE AND RETRIBUTION.[2]

(Introduction.)

THE Exalted One says:[3] (1-3)
Curses and blessings do not come through gates,[4] but man himself invites their arrival.[5] (4-11)

The reward of good and evil is like the shadow accompanying a body, and so it is apparent[6] that heaven and earth are possessed of crime-recording spirits. (12-28)

According to[7] the lightness or gravity of his transgressions,[8] the sinner's term of life is reduced. Not only is his term of life reduced, but poverty[9] also strikes him. Often he meets with calamity and misery.[9] His neighbors[10] hate him. Punishments and curses pursue him. Good luck shuns him. Evil stars threaten him; and when his term of life comes to an end, he perishes. (29-67)

Further, there are the three councilor[11] spirit-lords of the northern constellation,[12] residing above the heads of the people, recorders of men's crimes and sins,9 cutting off terms of from twelve years to a hundred days. (68-87)

Further, there are the three body-spirits13 that live within man's person. Whenever Kêng Shên day 14 comes, they ascend to the heavenly master 15 and inform him of men's crimes and trespasses. (88-110)

On the last day of the month the Hearth Spirit,16 too, does the same. (111-118)

Of all the offences which men commit, the greater ones cause a loss of twelve years, the smaller ones of a hundred days. These their offences, great as well as small, constitute some hundred affairs, and those who are anxious for life everlasting,17 should above all avoid them.18 (119-147)

(Moral Injunctions.)

The right way leads forward; the wrong way backward.19 (148-155)

Do not proceed on an evil path. (156-159)

Do not sin20 in secret.21 (160-163)

Accumulate virtue, increase merit. (164-167)

With a compassionate heart turn toward all creatures. (168-171)

Be faithful, filial, friendly, and brotherly.22
(172-175)

First rectify thyself and then convert others. (176-179)

Take pity on orphans, assist widows; respect the old, be kind to children. (180-187)

Even the multifarious insects, herbs, and trees should not be injured. (188-195)

Be grieved at the misfortune of others and rejoice at their good luck. (196-204)

Assist those in need, and rescue those in danger. (205-212)

Regard your neighbor's gain as your own gain, and regard your neighbor's loss as your own loss. (213-228)

Do not call attention to the faults of others, nor boast of your own excellence. (229-236)

Stay evil and promote goodness. (237-240)

Renounce much, accept little. (241-244)

Show endurance in humiliation and bear no grudge. (245-248)

Receive favors as if surprised.[23] (249-252)

Extend your help without seeking reward.
(253-257)

Give to others and do not regret or begrudge your liberality. (258-262)

(Blessings of the Good.)

Those who are thus, are good: people honor them; Heaven's Reason[24] gives them grace[25]; blessings and abundance follow them; all ill luck keeps away[26]; angel spirits guard them. Whatever they undertake will surely succeed, and even to spiritual saintliness[27] they may aspire.

(263-294)

Those who wish to attain heavenly saintliness, should perform one thousand three hundred good deeds, and those who wish to attain to earthly saintliness should perform three hundred good deeds. (295-316)

(A Description of Evil-Doers.)

Yet[28] there are some people whose behavior is unrighteous. (317-322)

Their deportment is irrational.[29] (323-326)

In evil they delight.[30] (327-330)

With brutality they do harm and damage.

(331-334)

Insidiously they injure the good and the law-abiding. (335-338)

Stealthily they despise their superiors and parents. (339-342)

They disregard their seniors and rebel against those whom they serve. (343-350)

They deceive the uninformed. (351-354)

They slander their fellow-students. (355-358)

Liars they are, bearing false witness, deceivers, and hypocrites; malevolent exposers of kith and kin[31]; mischievous and malignant; not humane; cruel and irrational; self-willed.

(359-374)

Right and wrong they confound. Their avowals and disavowals are not as they ought to be.[32] (375-382)

They oppress their subordinates and appropriate their merit. (383-386)

They cringe to superiors to curry favor. (387-390)

Insentient to favors received, they remember their hatred and are never satisfied.(391-398)

They hold in contempt the lives of Heaven's people.[33] (399-402)

They agitate and disturb the public order. (403-406)

They patronize the unscrupulous and do harm to the inoffensive. (407-413)

They murder men to take their property, or have them ousted to take their places.(414-422)

They slay the yielding and slaughter those who have surrendered. (423-426)

They malign the righteous and dispossess the wise. (427-430)

They molest orphans and wrong widows. (431-434)

Disregarders of law they are, and bribe takers. They call crooked what is straight, straight what is crooked, and what is light they make heavy. (435-450)

When witnessing an execution, they aggravate it by harshness. (451-454)

Though they know their mistakes they do not correct them; though they know the good they do not do it. (455-462)

In their own guilt they implicate others.34
(463-466)

They impede and obstruct the professions and crafts.35 (467-470)

They vilify and disparage the holy and the wise.(471-474)

They ridicule and scorn reason and virtue.36 (475-478)

They shoot the flying, chase the running, expose the hiding, surprise nestlings, close up entrance holes, upset nests, injure the pregnant, and break the egg. (479-494)

They wish others to incur loss. (495-498)

They disparage others that achieve merit.
(499-502)

They endanger others to save themselves.
(503-506)

They impoverish others for their own gain. (507-510)

For worthless things they exchange what is valuable. (511-514)

For private ends they neglect public duties. (515-518)

They appropriate the accomplishments of their neighbor and conceal his good qualities. They make known his foibles and expose his secrets. They squander his property and cause divisions in his family.37 (519-542)

They attack that which is dear to others. (543-547)

They assist others in doing wrong. (548-551)

Their unbridled ambition makes for power, and through the degradation of others they seek success. (552-558)

They desroy the crops and fields of others. (559-562)

They break up betrothals. (563-566)

Improperly they have grown rich, and withal they remain vulgar. (567-570)

Improperly they shirk38 without shame. (571-574)

They claim having done acts of favor and disclaim being at fault. (575-578)

They give away evil in marriage39 and they sell wrongs. (579-582)

They sell and buy vainglory. (583-586)

They conceal and keep a treacherous heart. (587-590)

They crush that which is excellent in others. (591-594)

They are careful in hiding their shortcomings. (595-598)

Being on a high horse they threaten and intimidate. (599-602)

With unrestrained barbarism they kill and stab. (603-606)

Recklessly they cut cloth to waste.40 (607-610)

Without festive occasions they prepare cattle for food.41 (611-614)

They scatter and waste the five cereals.42
(615-618)

They trouble and annoy many people.
(619-622)

They break into others' houses to take their property and valuables. (623-630)

They misdirect the water and light fires to destroy the people's homes. (631-638)

They upset others' plans so as to prevent their success. (639-646)

They spoil a worker's utensils to hamper his efficiency. (647-654)

When seeing the success and prosperity of others they wish them to run down and fail.
(655-662)

Seeing the wealth of others, they wish them bankrupt and ruined. (663-670)

They cannot see beauty without cherishing in their hearts thoughts of seduction. (671-678)

Being indebted to others for goods or property, they wish their creditors to die. (679-686)

When their requests are not granted they begin to curse and wax hateful. (687-694)

Seeing their neighbor lose his vantage they gossip of his failure. (695-702)

Seeing a man imperfect in his bodily features they ridicule him. (703-711)

Observing the talent and ability of a man worthy of praise, they suppress the truth.
(712-720)

They use charms43 for the sake of controlling others.44 (721-724)

They employ drugs to kill trees. (725-728)

Ill-humored and angry they are towards teachers and instructors. (729-732)

They resist and provoke father and elders.
(733-736)

With violence they seize, with violence they demand. (737-740)

They delight in fraud, they delight in robbery, they make raids and commit depredations to get rich. (741-748)

By artful tricks they seek promotion. (749-752)

They reward and punish without justice.
(753-756)

They indulge in comforts and enjoyments without measure. (757-761)

They harass and tyrannize over their subordinates. (762-765)

They terrify and threaten to overawe others. (766-768)

They accuse heaven and find fault with man. (769-772)

They blame the wind and rail at the rain. (773-776)

They stir up party strife and law suits. (777-780)

Unprovoked they join factious associations.45 (781-784)

They rely on their wives' and other women's gossip. (785-788)

They disobey the instructions of father and mother. (789-792)

They take up the new and forget the old. (793-796)

Their mouth asserts what their heart denies. (797-800)

Shamelessly greedy they are for wealth. (801-804)

They deceive their father and their superiors. (805-808)

They invent and circulate vile talk, traducing and slandering innocent men. (809-816)

They slander others, yet themselves feign honesty. (817-820)

They rail at spirits and claim to be right themselves. (821-824)

They reject a good cause and espouse a wrong cause, spurning what is near, longing for the distant.46 (825-832)

They point at heaven and earth[47] to make them witnesses of their mean thoughts. (833-839)

They even call on bright spirits to make them witness their degrading deeds. (840-846)

When they ever give charity they regret it afterwards. (847-850)

They borrow and accept without intention to return. (851-854)

Beyond their due lot they scheme and contrive. (855-858)

Above their means they plot and plan.

(859-862)

Their lusty desires exceed all measure.

(863-866)

Their heart is venomous while they show a compassionate face. (867-870)

With filthy food they feed the poor. (871-874)

With heresies they mislead others. (875-878)

They shorten the foot, they narrow the measure, they lighten the scales, they reduce the peck. (879-886)

They adulterate the genuine, and they seek profit[48] in illegitimate business. (887-894)

They compel respectable people to become lowly. (895-898)

They betray and deceive the simple-minded.

(899-902)

They are greedy and covetous without satiety. (903-906)

They curse and swear to seek vindication.
(907-910)

Indulging in liquor they become rebellious and unruly. (911-914)

With the members of their own family[37] they are angry and quarrelsome. (915-918)

As husbands[49] they are neither faithful nor kind. (919-922)

As wives[49] they are neither gentle nor pliant. (923-926)

As husbands they are not in harmony with their wives;[50] as wives they are not respectful to their husbands. (927-934)

As husbands they delight in bragging and conceit. (935-938)

Always as wives they practice jealousy and suspicion. (939-942)

As husbands they behave unmannerly toward their wives and children. (943-947)

As wives they lack propriety to their father-in-law and their mother-in-law. (948-952)

They make light of the spirit of their ancestor. (953-956)

They disobey and dislike the commands of their superiors. (957-960)

They make and do what is not useful.
(961-964)

They harbor and keep a treacherous[51] heart. (965-968)

They curse themselves[52], they curse others.
(969-972)

They are partial in their hatred and partial in their love. (973-976)

They step over the well and they step over the hearth. They jump over the food and jump over a person.[53] (977-984)

They kill the baby and cause abortion of the unborn. (985-988)

They do many clandestine and wrong deeds. (989-992)

The last day of the month and the last day of the year they sing and dance.[54]   The first day of the month, the first day of the year, they start roaring and scolding. (993-1000)

Facing the north, they snivel and spit; facing the hearth, they sing, hum and weep.[55]
(1001-1012)

Further, with hearth fire they burn incense,[56] and with filthy fagots they cook their food. (1013-1018)

In the night they rise and expose their nakedness.[57] (1019-1022)

On the eight festivals of the seasons they execute punishment.[58] (1023-1030)

They spit at falling stars and point at the many-colored rainbow.[59] (1031-1036)

Irreverently they point at the three luminaries;[60] intently they gaze at the sun and at the moon. (1037-1044)

In the spring they hunt with fire.[61] (1045-1048)

Facing the north, they use vile language.[55]
(1049-1052)

Causelessly they kill tortoises and snakes.
(1053-1058)

(Punishments for Evil-Doers.)

For all these crimes the councilors of destiny deprive the guilty, according to the lightness or gravity of the offence, of terms from twelve years to a hundred days, and when the lease of life is exhausted they perish. (1059-1076)

If at death an unexpiated offence be left, the evil luck will be transferred to children and grandchildren. (1077-1085)

Moreover, all those who wrongly seize others' property may have to compensate for it, with wives or children or other family members, the expiation to be proportionate up to a punishment by death. (1086-1106)

If the guilt be not expiated by death, they will suffer by various evils, by water, by fire, by theft, or by robbery, by loss of property, by disease and illness, and by ill repute, to compensate for any unlawful violence of justice.
(1107-1132)

Further, those who unlawfully kill men will in turn have their weapons and arms turned on them; yea, they will kill each other.[62] (1133-1145)

(A Simile.)

Those who seize property, are, to use an illustration, like those who relieve their hunger by eating tainted meat,[63] or quench their thirst by drinking poisoned liquor. Though they are not without temporary gratification, death will anon overcome them. (1146-1169)

(Good and Evil Spirits.)

If a man's heart be awakened to the good, though the good be not yet accomplished, good spirits verily are already following him.
(1170-1184)

If a man's heart be awakened to evil, though evil be not yet accomplished, evil spirits verily are already following him. (1185-1199)

(Quotations.[64])

Those who have hitherto done evil deeds should henceforth mend and repent. (1200-1209)

If evil be no longer practiced and good deeds done, and if in this way a man continues and continues, he will surely obtain happiness and felicity. He will, indeed, so to speak, transform curses into blessings. (1210-1230)

(Conclusion.)

Therefore, blessed is the man who speaketh what is good, who thinketh what is good, who practiceth what is good. If but each single day he would persevere in these three ways of goodness,[65] within three years Heaven will surely shower on him blessings. (1231-1251)

Unfortunate is the man who speaketh what is evil, who thinketh what is evil, who practiceth what is evil. If but each single day he would persevere in these three ways of evil-doing, within three years Heaven will surely shower on him curses. (1252-1271)

Why shall we not be diligent and comply with this? (1272-1277)

EXPLANATORY NOTES

EXPLANATORY NOTES.

[1] *T'ai-Shang,* "the Exalted One," also called *T'ai Shang Lao Chün,* "the Exalted Ancient Master," is an honorary appellation of *Li Er,* who is popularly known as *Lao Tze,* "the Ancient Philosopher."

[2] The title is commonly but not correctly translated "The Book of Rewards and Punishments."

For an explanation of the meaning of "Response and Retribution" see the Introduction.

[3] The word "says" can scarcely be construed to imply a claim that the treatise has been written by T'ai Shang, i. e., Lao Tze; it simply means that the doctrines here enunciated are his.

[4] The phrase, "have no gates," presents some difficulties. The obvious meaning is that curses and blessings are not limited to special avenues, on which they come down to mankind from heaven. There are no special doors in our houses through which they enter; they are independent of space and come in response to our actions. In other words, it is not blind fate that directs curses and blessings, but we ourselves are the forgers of our destiny. Curses and blessings come in exact proportion to man's merit or demerit. Following the sense rather than the words, Stanislas Julien translates: "Le malheur et le bonheur de

l'homme s'attire lui même l'un ou l'autre par sa con-
duite." He adds the following explanation: "L'expression *wou-men* (6-7) veut dire qu'il n'y a point
de porte ni de chemin déterminés d'avance par le
ciel, qui conduisent au bonheur ou au malheur."

⁵ The word "arrival" does not stand in the original
and is supplied by the context.

⁶ The two Chinese words here translated "therefore" are used (like the Latin *ergo*) to introduce a
logical conclusion. They imply that the preceding
statement is a proof for the truth of the following
assertion. Accordingly, we translate: " and so it is
apparent that...."

⁷ In the relative clause (words 29-34 of the Chinese
text) the preposition "proportionately to" belongs to
the nouns "lightness" and "gravity," and the whole relative clause, "man's of that in which he transgresses,"
is, in the Chinese, inserted. In such constructions we
have a palpable instance of the incommensurability
of the English and the Chinese grammars.

⁸ The character *i* is commonly translated by the
preposition "through," or "with," or "by." Here it
is used as an adverb "thereby," or "thus," which can
be omitted in English.

⁹ In Chinese all words are monosyllables, and as
there are more characters than sounds, the language
abounds in homophones, i. e., words which sound
alike but are written differently and have different
meanings. To avoid a misunderstanding, the Chinese
like to add a synonym to a doubtful word, so as to
make sure of the meaning. Thus they add to the
word "calamity" the word "trouble," which both to-

gether fuse into one idea, and there is no need of translating them by two terms. We have, as a rule, retained the Chinese mode of expressing one idea by two synonyms.

[10] The Chinese character commonly translated by "all" has not the full weight of the English equivalent. It may simply be translated by the plural form of the following noun.

[11] The three councilor spirits are represented in the starry heavens (according to Giles) by three stars (ι, κ, λ), according to Stanislas Julien by the six stars (ι, κ; λ, μ; ν, ξ) in the Great Bear. See Giles, *Chin. Dict.*, s. v. *Tai* = "councilor," Morrison, II, p. 1072, and the Chinese Encyclopædia, *San tsai tou hoei* I, fol. 12. (Stanislas Julien, *loc. cit.* p. 13.)

[12] That part of the constellation Ursa Major (the Great Bear), which is called "the Dipper" in the United States, is called "the Bushel" in China. On account of the conspicuous place which it holds in the sky, it is counted among the three measures of time, the other two being the sun and the moon; and it is commonly regarded as sacred.

[13] According to Chinese views, the vital functions of man's body are presided over by the three body-spirits called *san chi shên*. They are the upper chi, *Peng-Kiu;* the middle chi, *Peng-chi;* and the lower chi, *Peng-Kiao*. According to Basile's *Dictionnaire*, they reside in the head, the stomach, and the abdomen. (See Julien, *Le livre des récompenses*, p. 15.) Other authorities make different statements. See, e. g., Du Bose's *Dragon, Image and Demon*, pp. 395-396.

When a man falls asleep on Kêng-shên day, the

three body-spirits leave their habitation to bring the
Heavenly Master information concerning the sins
which they have witnessed. Hence originated the
practice of keeping vigils on Kêng-shên days so as
not to be found sleeping at the time of judgment, or
(as otherwise the custom is explained) to prevent the
three body-spirits from leaving the body.

[14] The Chinese calendar is a complicated affair.
The names of days are made up by a combination of
two words belonging to two different sets of names
one of which is called the Ten Stems and the other
the Twelve Branches. The Ten Stems are repeated
six times and the Twelve Branches five times, which
yields sixty combinations. The Kêng-shên day, the
day of judgment in the heavenly courts, is the fifty-
seventh day in this sexagesimal system. See for
further infomation Dr. Paul Carus' "Chinese Script
and Thought" in *The Monist*, April, 1905.

[15] The "Heavenly Master" is a Taoist term denoting the governor and judge of the world. He is
also called the "Pearly Emperor" and is identified
with "Shang Ti," the Lord on High.

[16] The hearth - spirit watches the events in the
house, and his day of reckoning is the last day of
every month, called *hwi* in Chinese, which we translate in our verbatim translation by "ultimo" in the
sense in which the word is used in continental Europe.

[17] The character "long life" practically means "immortality" in Chinese, and so we have here translated
it by "life everlasting." Stanislas Julien translates
"L'immortalité."

[18] Stanislas Julien translates this passage: "Il faut

d'avance les éviter avec soin, si l'on veut obtenir l'immortalité."

[19] The meaning of this sentence is that the right way is the one that leads onward. Stanislas Julien (*loc. cit.* p. 32) translates: "Avancez dans la bonne voie, et reculez devant la mauvaise voie." Legge (in the *S. B. E.,* Vol. XL, p. 237) translates: "Is his way right, he should go forward in it; is it wrong, he should withdraw from it." Mr. Suzuki insists that this interpretation though it makes excellent sense, is positively untenable.

[20] "To be false to oneself" means "to do wrong," or "to sin."

[21] "In the dark room" simply means "in secret."

[22] This sentence is a condensed statement of Confucian morality.

[23] This sentence is a modified quotation from Lao Tze's *Tao-Teh-King.* Lao Tze says (chap. 13): "Favor and disgrace bode awe." The Chinese word *ching,* which, following the traditional interpretation, (see Carus, *Lao Tze's Tao-Teh-King,* p. 163) means "fearful surprise," or "awe," is the same that here simply means "surprise." We need not add that by the omission of the word "disgrace" the sense is somewhat altered. Yet, after all, the meaning of the word combination "favor and disgrace" does not so much mean "favor" and also "disgrace," but a condition of dependence, such as prevails in court life, where "favor and disgrace" are the significant features. It is an instance of an idea expressed in Chinese by the contrast of two opposites of which the idea consists.

[24] For the word *tao* see Carus' *Lao Tze's Tao-Teh-*

King, pp. 9 ff. and xxii-xxvi. The word *tao* is in one
respect unlike its equivalent in English which we translate by "reason." It is a religious term with which is
associated all the awe for the sanctity of the moral
world-order, such as is attached to its Greek equivalent, the word *logos* or "word," i. e., "logical thought."

²⁵ Stanislas Julien translates: "La providence le
protége."

²⁶ "Tous les démons s'éloignent de lui."

²⁷ The word "saint" consists of the symbols "man"
and "mountain." The Man of the Mountain was a
hermit or recluse, and so the word acquired the meaning "saint." The etymological significance, though still
noticeable in its etymology, is, however, lost sight of,
and the word now simply means, "saint" or "saintly."
According to Eitel (*Handbook of Buddhism,* p. 130),
there are five degrees of saintliness: heavenly, ærial,
human, earthly, and ghostly. In the present passage
only two degrees of saintliness are referred to.

²⁸ All the following sentences are dependent upon
this conjunction *Kou,* i. e., "if," in this way: "*If* some
people do not behave righteously, (*if*) they are un-
reasonable, (*if*) they take pride in evil, (*if*) they in-
flict wounds," etc., etc., down to the last sentence of
"*a description of evil-doers.*" The main sentence begins with the part entitled "Punishment of Evil-Doers"
with the words (1059 ff.): "for such crimes the con-
trollers of destiny cut short people's lives." We break
up this long-winded construction to render our English version more readable.

²⁹ The word "reason" is not here the same as *tao,*
mentioned above, but *li,* which means "logical correct-

ness" or "rationality," i. e., "reason," in a secular sense. The meaning of the sentence here is that unrighteousness is not only against the *tao,* i. e., against religion, but even against common sense.

[30] Stanislas Julien translates: "Regarder la méchanceté comme une preuve de talent."

[31] M. Julien translates this sentence: "Divulger les fautes de ses parens."

[32] Stanislas Julien translates: "Ne pas savoir distinguer les personnes qu'il faut rechercher ou fuir."

[33] The expression "heaven's people" is a Confucian term, which is used in China in the same way as in Christian countries the phrase "God's people" would mean all those who bear God's image and are dear to the Deity.

[34] M. Julien translates: "Rejeter ses propres crimes sur les autres."

[35] The words *Fang-Shu,* here rendered "divination" and "craft," denote first of all the practice of diviners; but it is here used in a general sense and applies to all skilled labor, especially the professions. M. Julien translates: "Arrêter l'exercice des arts et des métiers." He adds in a footnote: "According to the dictionary of the Fo Kien dialect, the *Fang-Shu* are (1) physicians, (2) men of letters, (3) painters, (4) diviners, (5) journalists, (6) merchants, (7) workmen, (8) fishers, and (9) woodcutters." (*Ibid.* p. 221.) For further information in regard to the Feng-Shui, see Dr. Carus' article "Chinese Occultism" in *The Monist,* Vol. XV, p. 500.

[36] "Reason and virtue," i. e., *tao* and *teh,* are the two main subjects of Lao Tze's doctrine. We are at

liberty to translate "reason and virtue," or "the way of virtue."

37 The term "bone and flesh" in Chinese means "family relations."

38 The meaning may be either "to escape punishment" or "to shirk duties."

39 "To give away evil in marriage" is a Chinese phrase.

40 Literally, "they cut and clip," which is a term in tailoring. The meaning of the sentence is that they are wasteful with material, and it goes without saying that it refers to wastefulness of any kind.

41 It is customary in China to kill cattle on festivals only, and it is considered improper and even irreligious to slay cattle for food without due occasion.

42 Wilful waste of food is rightly considered sinful in China.

43 Among the Chinese superstitions which are common also in other countries, is the habit of burying figures or worms, which are intended to represent some person, for the purpose of inflicting injury upon them, being a kind of black magic. This is callled in Chinese "to bury vermin."

44 Stanislas Julien translates: "Cacher l'effigie d'un homme pour lui donner le cauchemar."

45 Associations or fraternities have always played an important part in Chinese politics. The Boxer movement is a well-known instance in modern times.

46 M. Julien translates: "Tourner le dos à ses proches parens et rechercher ses parens éloignés."

⁴⁷ To point at heaven and earth or the stars is deemed disrespectful in China, and the habit of making them witnesses of mean thoughts is considered a defiance of the divine powers.

⁴⁸ "Illegitimate profit" refers to the business not licensed by the authorities, such as was the opium trade before the Opium War.

⁴⁹ The following sentences refer alternately to husbands and wives, which for clearness' sake has to be repeated in English.

⁵⁰ Literally, "the room," viz., the one in which the wife lives. Denoting the sphere of the wife's activity, the word has become a synonym for "wife."

⁵¹ Literally, "outside." An outside heart means a "treacherous heart."

⁵² According to the rules of Chinese grammar, the objective case of "self" precedes the verb.

⁵³ It is considered disrespectful in China to step over the well, the hearth, food, or a person.

⁵⁴ While the Chinese celebrate New Year's Eve as much as is done in Western countries, the custom to sing and to dance on such festivals is considered highly improper.

⁵⁵ No act that may be regarded as disrespectful should be done while facing the North, and also in presence of the hearth which is the most sacred place of the house.

⁵⁶ The proper way to light incense in olden times was to strike a spark from a flint. To burn incense in the fire of the hearth is both disrespectful for the hearth and improper so far as the incense is concerned.

⁵⁷ The command "not to expose one's nakedness in the night," is based upon an ancient notion, (viz., that spirits, angels, or demons may have intercourse with human beings,) a remnant of which is still preserved in the Old Testament (Gen. vi. 2), where we read that the sons of Elohim took to wives the daughters of men. One of the Chinese stories appended to the *T'ai-Shang Kan-Ying P'ien* tells of a woman that conceived a changeling from a demon, and the Apostle Paul, for the same reason that underlies the notion of our present passage in the *T'ai-Shang Kan-Ying P'ien*, requests women to wear a head covering (1 Cor. xi. 10).

⁵⁸ It is considered as irreligious to have executions take place on festivals, a custom which is paralleled in the Jewish law, according to which it is unlawful to have a man stoned or crucified on the feast day.

⁵⁹ The word "rainbow" is here as in many other places represented by two words, the second of which means literally "colored cloud." See Note 9.

⁶⁰ The three luminaries (or more correctly the three kinds of luminaries) are sun, moon, and stars.

⁶¹ Hunting by setting the underbrush on fire in spring when animals begin to hatch, is rightly denounced as cruel in China.

⁶² I understand the sentence, "those who slay, exchange weapons," to mean that "he that killeth with the sword must be killed with the sword" (Rev. xiv. 10); and further, adds the Chinese moralist in the following sentence, "such evil-doers will turn their swords against one another and mutually kill them-

selves," which is a gradation, for it is stated that not only will they be killed, but they will slay one another.

⁶³ Meat that has by carelessness been exposed to the water dripping from the eaves has frequently proved fatal to those who partook of it. Thus the term "dripping water meat" means "tainted meat."

⁶⁴ These passages are quotations from the *Dhammapada* which has become a household book of religious devotion all over China.

⁶⁵ The threefold way of good thoughts, good words, and good deeds, is a proposition which, so far as we know, was first taught in the West by Zarathushtra, the great prophet of Iran.

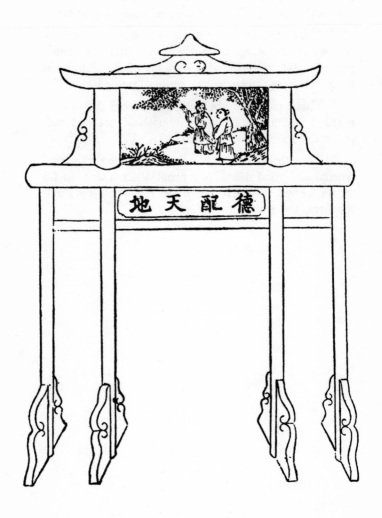

MORAL TALES

ILLUSTRATIVE OF THE KAN-YING P'IEN

MORAL TALES ILLUSTRATIVE OF THE KAN-YING P'IEN .

RAYS OF TRUTH.

A COPY of the *T'ai-Shang Kan-Ying P'ien* had been handed down in the family of Wan Teh-Hsü from one of his ancestors as a very precious heirloom. Four successive generations had reverently read and recited it, and now when it came into the possession of Wan Teh-Hsü, he kept it in a place of honor in the Middle Hall; and he, and all the members of his family, had many merits recorded in their favor, for they vied with one another in living up to the moral principles laid down in the sacred document.

One day a Taoist priest visited the home of the pious man and was cordially received. Wan Teh-Hsü presented his guest with gifts and requested him to discourse on the mystery of religion, whereupon the stranger expounded the Tao, that divine rationality which pervades all things.

"The soul," he said. "is Tao, and the Tao
is soul. The soul and the Tao are not different
in essence. If the Tao is separated from the
soul, you will transmigrate through the six
domains and keep on the three paths,* but if
the soul and the Tao are united, you will finally
reach paradise and the land of immortals. Hell
and heaven are in your own heart. Unless
heaven reside within you, the mere reading
or reciting of sacred books profiteth nothing."
Then looking around in the Middle Hall he
added: "You have a rare gem in your house;
for when I entered I saw the radiance of a
holy light. Where do you keep your treasure?"

The host answered: "In this poor dwelling
there is nothing worthy the name of a treasure."

The priest then took Wan Teh-Hsü by the
hand and led him to the place where the *Kan
Ying P'ien* lay, saying: "This holy book is the
treasure. All the holy men of the three reli-
gions selected and compiled it to point out the
way of virtue on which every one should walk.
If a man disciplines himself according to its
instructions, the truth will shine forth in all

* The six domains are those of (1) the gods, (2) human
beings, (3) animals, (4) *asuras* or fighting demons, (5)
hungry ghosts, and (6) denizens of hell. The three paths are
lust, wrath, and greed. The three paths and the six domains
constitute the wheel of Samsara.

WELCOMED IN HEAVEN.

its glory, and every letter in the sacred writing will emit rays of divine light. But if you recite the sacred text with a secret desire for profit or reward, selfishness will darken its native glory, and the writing will show no illumination. To my vision the glorification of the holy book is perfect. Its saintly atmosphere has ascended to heaven, resulting in an harmonious blending of your heart with the will of the Lord on High. Your immortality is assured and I bless you. But keeping in sight the heavenly station that awaits you, you must continue to exercise still more self-control in your dealings with your fellow men. Be diligent and fail not to fulfil the work so auspiciously begun."

In accordance with the words of the Taoist priest, Teh-Hsü practiced the teachings of the *Kan-Ying P'ien* with even greater zeal. For thirty more years, he did everything in his power to benefit others and to promote general welfare. One day his neighbors heard heavenly music resound from above, and saw the entire family of Wan ascend to heaven in broad daylight, surrounded by a host of celestial beings.

Later the villagers built a monument to Wan on his own homestead, where they paid him homage and offered prayers which were answered and granted.

[Our illustration shows Ti Chün, the Lord Superior (also called Wen Chang, the patron god of the Taoist religion) accompanied by two attendants, welcoming the good man and his family as they are carried up to heaven. Below we see the neighbors, some of them on their knees, witnessing the scene.]

THE PIOUS SCHOLAR'S GOOD FORTUNE.

Shang Shih-Ying of the Ming dynasty was a good caligrapher. Though poor, he was diligent in doing good. Once he saw a man asking for aid to print and distribute the *Kan-Ying P'ien*. He wanted to help the man, and having no means, pawned his clothing. With the cash thus realized he gratified his pious desire, but on this account had to go without warm clothing in winter. Even when he was thirty years of age, he was as poor as ever. He went to the capital to try his fortune, but nobody seemed to recognize his abilities. To gain a living he was obliged to compose and copy for other people, poems which were to be dedicated to Kwang Ti.

New Year's Eve was approaching and the chief mandarin had some official business to attend to at the shrine of Kwang Ti. He sent one of his clerks who was a man of good judgment, and he greatly admired the work of Shang, hung up in the shrine, and asked the poor scholar to accompany him home as a guest of honor.

On the night of the fifteenth of January, the festival of lanterns, the chief mandarin, according to custom, decorated his garden and tested the poetical and calligraphic skill of his invited friends in competitive games, the best compositions to be attached to the lanterns. Since the result was not very satisfactory, the clerk recommended the poor scholar who stayed at his house. Shang was at once summoned and his unusual talents were admired by the whole company.

It happened that evening that the Emperor came to inspect the illumination, and he was greatly impressed by the beautiful handwriting of the inscriptions. He had their author presented to him, and recognizing his worth, conferred a high literary degree upon him.

From that time, Shang's promotion was rapid till he was honored with the highest literary title and occupied the very important position of secretary to the Emperor.

One day after his regular work at the Court, he went to the shrine of Kwang Ti to give thanks for his prosperity. The priest re-

ceived him very cordially, and when the cere-
mony was over, let him take a rest in the
temple when lo, Kwang Ti appeared to him
in his ethereal form and said: "The prosperity
you are enjoying to-day is the result of your
meritorious work in helping others print and
distribute the *Kan-Ying P'ien*. Keep on culti-
vating piety in your heart as before, be loyal
and faithful to your superiors as well as to the
State, and never think of abusing the power
which is yours at present."

Coming to know the reason of his unparalleled success in life, he advised others to follow
his example and made many converts.

[The reader of this story should know that Kwang
Ti, the war god, is not merely the Chinese Mars, but
presides generally over the affairs of mortals. He may
be compared to St. Peter or the Archangel Michael.

In the illustration, the inscription over the entrance of the temple reads literally: "All the heavens
together are filled with glory," reminding us of the
beginning of the nineteenth Psalm: "The heavens de-
clare the glory of God." The inscription reading
downwards on the column is a loose quotation from
the *Kan-Ying P'ien*: "Lucky stars follow the good
man."]

THE PIOUS SCHOLAR'S GOOD FORTUNE.

PHILANTHROPY REWARDED.

The people in the province of Chiang-Hsi had an objection to raising daughters, and on that account there were a great many bachelors there. The governor wanted to put a stop to the inhuman custom of drowning infants, and so he summoned some of his old councilors to see what measures could best be taken to effect this. Old state documents were consulted and it appeared that many of the preceding governors had attempted the same reform but had signally failed. So the task seemed to be beset with insurmountable difficulties.

After a meeting with his councilors the governor retired, still thinking that there must be some method which would effectively put an end to the barbarous practice, and he thought, what could cause people to suppress parental love but the expense and trouble they must undergo at the time of giving their daughters in marriage. If there were built a sort of public nursery where all the female children could be provided for by the state, the cruelty of drowning girls would naturally cease.

While going over the old records, the governor had found that there were deserted temples and shrines to which a regular annual revenue was still attached. He thought these revenues might be used with great benefit to the public. In the morning he would go to the temple of the Heavenly Mother and ask her gracious assistance for this scheme.

That same night the priest of the temple was informed in a dream by the Heavenly Mother concerning the governor's humane project and his impending visit in the morning. She added that though his philanthropic scheme had not yet been executed, the very thought of lovingkindness that prompted it, had caused a commotion in heaven and he was attended by a host of angels.

According to the divine command, every preparation was made in the temple to receive the governor. After due salutation, the priest inquired whether his mission was about the establishment of a nursery. The governor was greatly surprised to find him well informed in regard to the secret plan which had not been divulged to anybody. The priest then told him all about the previous night's communication from the Heavenly Mother.

The benevolent plan was successfully put into execution and general prosperity began

PHILANTHROPY REWARDED.

to reign in the district. The governor was promoted by the Emperor and died at an advanced age, surrounded by his children who were all prosperous and respected.

THE POWER OF A GOOD MAN'S NAME.

King Tsing, while on his way to a large gathering, passed through a district called Chun-Hoa, where there lived a young girl who was possessed of evil spirits. When King passed the night at her home, the demons did not dare to enter, but they returned as soon as he left the house. The young girl asked them the reason and they answered, "We are afraid of King." She then told her father who ran after King Tsing to call him back. But the good man simply wrote these four words on a slip of paper: *King Tsing tsaï tzu* ("King Tsing is here"), and advised him to paste it on the door. The demons never dared to return.

This true story goes to prove that the presence of a good man can put evil spirits to flight.

[This story encourages the use of charms and incantations, but it reveals to us the logic of exorcism. If the presence of a good man keeps demons away, the same result might be effected in his absence, if the de-

mons can be made to believe that the good man whom
they fear is actually present.

It is a common belief that the mere name of a
person or god is as efficient as its owner, and hence
is to be kept sacred. In this way, according to the faith
of the early Christians, miracles are performed in the
name of Jesus.]

GOOD SPIRITS IN ATTENDANCE.

Yuen, having conceived a violent hatred
against an acquaintance, set out one morning,
knife in hand, with the purpose of killing him.
A venerable man sitting in a convent saw him
pass, and was amazed to observe several scores
of spirits closely following him, some of whom
clutched his weapon, while others seemed en-
deavoring to delay his progress. About the
space of a meal-time the patriarch noticed
Yuen's return, accompanied this time by more
than a hundred spirits wearing golden caps
and bearing banners raised on high. Yuen himself appeared with so happy a face, in place of
his gloomy countenance of the early morning,
that the old man sadly concluded that his enemy must be dead and his revenge gratified.

"When you passed this way at daybreak,"
he asked, "where were you going, and why
do you return so soon?"

"It was owing to my quarrel with Miu,"

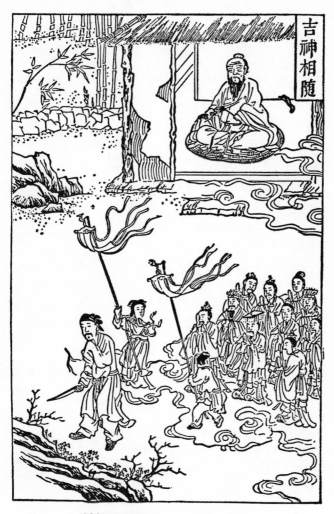

GOOD SPIRITS IN ATTENDANCE.

said Yuen, "that made me wish to kill him.
But in passing this convent door better
thoughts came to me as I pondered upon the
distress his wife and children would come to,
and of his aged mother, none of whom had
done me wrong. I determined then not to
kill him, and return thus promptly from my
evil purpose."

It hardly needed the sage's commendations
to increase the reformed murderer's inner con-
tentment, imparted by the train of ghostly
helpers; he continued on his way rejoicing.

[This story, reproduced from Williams' *Middle
Kingdom,* is not contained in the moral tales annexed
to the *Kan-Ying P'ien* but is taken from a similar
collection following the *Sacred Edict of Kang-Hi.*
Its insertion here is justified since it illustrates a quotation from the *Kan-Ying P'ien* (1184-1188) which
is almost literal and is inscribed in a corner of the
picture.]

A RUFFIAN'S REFORM.

Wu Chien-Chiu of Shan-Yu had wonder-
ful muscular strength, and nobody in his town
could beat him at boxing or fencing. He became so overbearing that any person who dared
affront him was sure to pay a penalty for it.
He borrowed the property of others without
ever returning it, and he compelled people to

do things for him under threats of severe punishment.

One summer evening he went up to the tower to cool off in the breeze. When the people who had gathered there saw the ruffian come they ran away, except one old man who seemed quite indifferent to his presence.

"Why do you alone dare defy my power?" cried Wu, intending to intimidate the old gentleman, but the latter replied:

"How profound your ignorance is! Your mother's womb sheltered you for ten long months, and your mother's arms took tender care of you for three more years. Your parents wanted you to grow and mature into a good, serviceable citizen of the Empire. When you would achieve something for the State, your family name would become known and glorified. You have undoubtedly some unusual talents. Why, then, degrade yourself thus and become the useless fellow you are now? The State loses in you a serviceable citizen, and the spirits of your parents feel disgusted with you. This is greatly to be deplored."

Wu felt so much ashamed that he had a chill of cold perspiration, and he said: "The people have marked me as a desperate character, and I have acted accordingly; but by

A RUFFIAN'S REFORM.

your words I realize my predicament; pray tell me how to retrieve my good name."

The old gentleman replied: "You know the story of the butcher who became a saintly Buddhist at the instant when he repented and dropped the knife. Follow his example. If you repent and start on a righteous march onward, you will certainly become a just man and command the respect of others."

Wu was serious in his reform and having joined the army was finally promoted to the rank of general.

THE IMPIOUS MAGISTRATE.

Wang An-shih, a high magistrate of the Sung dynasty (960-1278 A. D.), was a learned scholar but recklessly irreverent, and so introduced radical innovations in his administration. People complained, officers demurred, and the emperor expressed surprise; but he would say, "Heavenly omens should not be heeded, human discontent need not be minded, and there is no sense in following the ancestral laws." He and his son, who assisted him in his office, even attempted to revive the ancient cruel custom of corporal punishment; but before the law was passed, the son died, and

Wang An-shih built a Buddhist temple on the site of his son's residence.

While the magistrate was performing the customary Buddhist rite, he thought he faintly perceived in the flame of a burning candle the image of his son, bound hand and foot in a cangue,* crying: "Our attempt to revive corporal mutilation angered Heaven, and I have no chance of getting out of this infernal torture."

Later An-shih fell in disgrace; he lost his position and died miserably in exile.

Now it happened that soon afterwards, one of An‑shih's relatives was taken ill, and swooned, and when he recovered, he said that he had been ushered into a special department in hell, where hung the sign: "Wickedness and Crime Eternally Prohibited," and there he saw a noble-looking man in a cangue, who had gray hair and large eyes. Though he did not mention the name of this unfortunate person, every one around knew that it was Wang An-shih of whom he spoke. When An-shih's daughter inquired what could be done, the sick man simply said: "All that is necessary is to accumulate merits and nothing more."

[Our illustration shows the vision in which the magistrate's son is seen to suffer. The inscription

* The Chinese pillory.

永禁奸邪

酆都城

THE IMPIOUS MAGISTRATE.

above the door reads, translated verbatim, "Eternally Prohibited Depravities and Crimes," which means that here is the department for punishing evil-doers of this class.

A CHRISTIAN CONCEPTION OF HELL.

It is interesting to notice that the Chinese conception of the maws of hell which has apparently developed quite independently of Christian influence, is nevertheless, practically the same. This may be seen by a comparison of the lower part of the illustrations of this story and the next with the typical conception of hell as held in Christendom during the Middle Ages. Our picture is a reproduction of a German woodcut made at the time of the Reformation, but similar representations can be met with in the literature of the same age in other Christian countries. One of these appears on the main entrance of the Cathedral of Bourges, France (Carus, *History of the Devil,* p. 181). The Chinese conception was directly derived from India, indirectly from Babylon, and the Christian view can be traced to the same source.]

A VISIT TO HELL.

Ch'üan Ju-Yü of Pu-Hai was a poor man, but he was never tired of doing every good and charitable work in his power. He also employed himself indefatigably, although he was often in poor health, in copying many good books to be distributed among his neighbors. When he was asked why he exerted himself so much in spite of his physical weakness, he replied that he was not trying to seek any reward, but simply wanted to give relief to his mind, which could not be kept idle for one moment.

One day he went to sea, and encountering a strong gale, found himself stranded on a

A VISIT TO HELL.

lonely island.   The scenery was very beautiful
and he was full of joy, when suddenly there appeared to him a Taoist scholar who said: "The
world delights in hypocrisy, but the Lord on
High praises sincerity.   You have hitherto
done good work in distributing sound moral
tractates, and this not for the sake of courting
a good opinion of yourself from others, but
simply from pure unaffected good-will.   So
much the more praiseworthy are your deeds in
the eyes of our Lord. Many scholars are clever
enough, yet they do not employ their talents
for the true cause; they abuse them in writing
immoral, seditious books; but they are now
suffering in the infernal regions the consequences brought on them by their own acts.
I shall take you there and let you see by way
of contrast how much better your fate is."

Then they went through space to that
strangest of lands.   The Taoist explained
everything they saw there. All kinds of torture were being applied to those immoral wri-
ters, who, while in the world, stirred up man's
beastly nature and allured many good people
to an early downfall.   The stranger also
showed him a stately-looking man in the
palace, who had been a good, upright officer
when on earth, punishing every crime that
tended to disturb social and political peace,

and was now superintending this department in the world below.

When the visit was over, the Taoist scholar brought Ch'üan back to the same island, where he secured a sailboat and finally succeeded in reaching his home. Ever since, he is wont to tell his neighbors how horrible the scene was which he had seen on his visit to hell.

[The peculiar attraction of this story is in its parallelism to Dante's Inferno. The Chinese characters over the entrance of hell are, *Feng Tu Cheng*, which means verbatim "The Inferno's Fortified Castle." The last two characters, taken as one word, form the common term for capital, and so we might translate it briefly by "The Capital of Hell."

In the upper right hand corner we see King Yama, the sovereign of the under world, seated on a throne with one of his attendants.]

MISUSE OF BOOKS.

A temple in the district of Wu-Kung-Hien contained a library which students from the district school often consulted. One winter day, four of them used some of the sacred books for fuel to heat the room, while another burned one book to warm some water for his toilet. Only one of their number, Kang Tui-Shan by name, was indignant at their conduct, but he dared not offer a word of censure.

The next night Kang Tui-Shan had a dream in which he and his fellow - students were led before the tribunal of the three divine Lord-Superior Magistrates.* The six prostrated themselves and one of the gods said: "Buddha is a great saint, why have you dared burn his sacred books to warm yourselves?"

The four students struck their foreheads against the ground and besought pardon for their crime, but were condemned to death. The one who warmed water for his toilet was doomed never to receive any advancement during his life. Finally the god asked Kang Tui-Shan why he had not remonstrated with his companions.

"I knew that they were doing wrong," answered Kang, "but as they are my elders, I was afraid my reproaches would offend them."

"I will pardon you," said the god, "but when you have risen to a prominent position do not fail to give your support and protection to the religion of Buddha."

When he awoke Kang wrote down his

---

* The name of this divine tribunal is Shen San-Kuan Ti Chün, which, literally translated, means the Divine Trinity of Official Lord Superiors. They are the gods of heaven, of earth, and of water. Their birthdays are celebrated on the fifteenth of the first, seventh, and tenth months, respectively. The first distributes blessings, the second forgives sins, and the third saves from fire.

dream.   He obtained the degree of *Chwang-Yüen** when the four other students failed in their examinations and were excluded from the contest.   Six months later the plague spread in their country and all four perished with their families, while the student who burned the sacred books to heat water was still, in his old age, merely a poor schoolmaster. He died from starvation in the seventh year of the reign of Shih-Tsung of the Ming dynasty (A. D. 1529).

Now it is a greater sin to waste sacred books than to mock and slander sages and saints.   Paper, whether written or printed, often contains maxims that wise men have bequeathed on us. If we use it for unclean purposes, if we trample it underfoot, instead of carefully preserving it, we are committing a crime as serious as if we slandered them.

[This respect for books is not peculiar to the Chinese. Among Western authors, Milton in his "Areopagitica" on the freedom of the press, uses very vigorous language, saying:

"Books are not absolutely dead things, but do contain a potency of life in them to be as active as that soul was whose progeny they are; nay, they do preserve as in a vial the purest efficacy and extraction of that living intellect that bred them. I know they are as lively, and as vigorously productive, as those

* The first rank in the list of doctors.

fabulous dragon's teeth, and, being sown up and down,
may chance to spring up armed men. And yet, on the
other hand, unless wariness be used, as good almost
kill a man as kill a good book: who kills a man kills
a reasonable creature, God's image; but he who de-
stroys a good book kills reason itself, kills the image
of God, as it were, in the eye. Many a man lives a
burden to the earth; but a good book is the precious
life-blood of a master-spirit, embalmed and treasured
up on purpose to a life beyond life. It is true, no
age can restore a life, whereof, perhaps, there is no
great loss; and revolutions of ages do not oft recover
the loss of a rejected truth, for the want of which
whole nations fare the worse."]

PUNISHMENT APPORTIONED TO CRIME.

In the garden of the city of Sieu-Shui-
Siuen, there once lived a man by the name of
Fan Ki, who led a wicked life. He induced
men to stir up quarrels and lawsuits with each
other, to seize by violence what did not belong
to them, and to dishonor other men's wives
and daughters. When he could not succeed
easily in carrying out his evil purposes, he
made use of the most odious stratagems.

One day he died suddenly, but came back
to life twenty-four hours afterward and bade
his wife gather together their relatives and
neighbors. When all were assembled he told
them that he had seen the king of the dark

realm who said to him, "Here the dead receive punishment for their deeds of evil. The
living know not the lot that is reserved for
them. They must be thrown into a bed of
coals whose heat is in proportion to the extent
of their crimes and to the harm they have done
their fellows."

The assembled company listened to this
report as to the words of a feverish patient;
they were incredulous and refused to believe
the story. But Fan Ki had filled the measure
of crime, and Yama, the king of hell, had de-
cided to make an example of him so as to
frighten men from their evil ways. At Yama's
command Fan Ki took a knife and mutilated
himself, saying, "This is my punishment for
inciting men to dissolute lives." He put out
both his eyes, saying, "This is my punishment
for having looked with anger at my parents,
and at the wives and daughters of other men
with guilt in my heart." He cut off his right
hand, saying, "This is my punishment for having killed a great number of animals." He cut
open his body and plucked out his heart, saying, "This is my punishment for causing others to die under tortures." And last of all he
cut out his tongue to punish himself for lying
and slandering.

The rumor of these occurrences spread

PUNISHMENT APPORTIONED TO CRIME.

afar, and people came from every direction to see the mangled body of the unhappy man. His wife and children were overcome with grief and shame, and closed the door to keep out the curious crowd. But Fan Ki, still living by the ordeal of Yama, said in inarticulate sounds, "I have but executed the commands of the king of hell, who wants my punishment to serve as a warning to others. What right have you to prevent them from seeing me?"

For six days the wicked man rolled upon the ground in the most horrible agonies, and at the end of that time he died.

This story teaches us what punishments are in store for evil-doers. How dare men act contrary to what they know to be just and right!

[This story is taken from Julien's French version, but the Chinese edition at our command contains a similar, though less detailed, story of self-mutilation, for the illustration of which the accompanying picture was originally used.]

THE NORTHERN CONSTELLATION.

P'ang Hêng - Hsiu organized with his friends an association the purpose of which was to worship the Northern Constellation. He observed all necessary religious disciplines and recited the *sutras* with reverence. One day, however, he became so intoxicated that he forgot himself. He stripped off his garments and slept facing the north. Waking up in the night, he showed his disrespect toward the constellation, when suddenly he heard a series of thunderclaps in the northwestern quarter, and lo! the gate of heaven was thrown wide open. Awed by this unexpected turn of affairs, P'ang hastily put on his clothing and was at the point of paying due homage to the Lord, when a god with dark face and dragonlike whiskers, carrying a golden rod in his hand, came down from above. He severely censured P'ang for his offence, saying: "You have organized a religious society yourself and are well aware of the sacred laws. Therefore, your violation of them becomes doubly punishable."

P'ang humbly begged for divine mercy, excusing his deportment by the temporary derangement of his mind.

The god said: "The reason why men of good behavior are free from blame, is that they never relax their moral vigilance at any moment. Remember the story of Ch'ü Pai-Yü who at night passed by the royal palace, yet he dismounted from his carriage as was customary to do in the daytime, and paid proper

THE NORTHERN CONSTELLATION.

reverence to the Imperial house. People are
still praising his unparalleled sincerity. Even
in darkness men must not unbridle themselves
and yield to their wanton passions. We will
let you go at present, but you will have to
suffer for your offence later on in life by re-
ceiving some civil punishment."

Ever since, P'ang shut himself up in his
house and did not dare to go outside lest some
misfortune should befall him. But how could
a poor mortal escape heavenly ordained punishment? One day he received an invitation
from one of his honorable relatives who had
just been promoted to an eminent official position at the capital. He accepted gladly and
went to the capital. While there, he went out
and in at pleasure. Once he passed by an
Imperial shrine, and, not knowing the official
regulations, kept on riding apace. Thereupon
the guard of the shrine arrested him for the
offence, and the judge sentenced him to one
hundred stripes. P'ang then came to realize
the significance of the divine prophecy.

[The Northern Constellation, called in Chinese
"the Bushel" and in Western countries "Ursa Major,"
is sacred to Ti Chün, (the Lord Superior), and any
intentional irreverence shown to it is regarded as disrespect toward the good Lord himself. Our illustra-

tion shows a messenger of Ti Chün stepping forth
from the gate of heaven to warn the trespasser.]

THE INCENSED GODDESS.

There was a shrine to the water-goddess
in the village of Ch'ing Ch'i, and her image
that was placed there was so nicely carved
that it looked like a real goddess of splendid
beauty. The villagers made her the guardian
of the district and paid her great respect.

It was the second month of the year when
the pear-blossoms on the grounds were very
pretty, that a party of young students was
passing by and admired the flowers. One of
them lifted the curtain that was hung before
the image of the goddess and exclaimed: "How
lovely she is! If she were alive I would make
her my mistress!"

His friends were shocked, but he laughed
at their scruples, saying that spirits and gods
have no reality; that it is well enough for the
people to believe in and fear them, because
such superstition made them the more amen-
able. He then composed a libelous poem and
wrote it on the wall, but his friends did not
say anything more, knowing the uselessness
of their advice.

After this they all went to the examination

THE INCENSED GODDESS.

hall, and stayed at the Wên Chang Dormitory. One evening the Lord Wên Chang* appeared to them in a dream, and they were greatly afraid to be in the presence of his august majesty. He had a roll on his table and declared to them: "As you know well, any student who is guilty of trifling with women is excluded from the list. Even a plain, ordinary woman should be respected by you; and how much more this is true of a holy goddess, you all must know. According to a report I have received it seems there is one of your number who has insulted the goddess of Ch'ing Ch'i." Having ascertained the name of the offender, the Lord cancelled it from the list, adding that this was done because the man was guilty of wronging a woman.

When the students met the following morning, they learned that each had the same dream during the night. Yet the offender himself was obdurate and said: "What has the Lord of Literature to do with such trifles? What harm can an image of clay do to me?"

He entered an examination cell, and having written down his seven essays with unusual vigor and brilliancy, felt assured of his

* Wên Chang means "Scripture Glory" and he bears the title Ti-Chün, "Lord Superior." He is worshiped all over China as the god of written revelation and is the patron of all educational institutions.

final success. But when the night was far
advanced, there appeared before him the goddess of water with her attendants. She censured him for both his grave offence and im-
penitence, and then ordered her maids to strike
him with their sticks until the student lost his
mind and destroyed all of his papers. When
he was carried out of the cell in the morning,
he was unconscious and died soon.

[The accompanying picture illustrates the examination hall where every candidate is seated in a sepa-
rate cell. The row in the corner is inscribed with the
words, "Heaven - Character Number," which means
"number one." In explanation we have to state that
one way of counting in Chinese is according to the
words of the Thousand Character Book, *Chien Tzu
Wen*, which begins with the words *Tien ti hsüan
huang*. This book is used as a primer in Chinese
schools, and every partly educated Chinaman knows
it by heart. It contains the thousand most important
characters used in daily life and no two characters are
alike. Thus, *tien* (heaven) means "one," *ti* (earth)
means "two," *hsüan* (dark) means "three," *huang*
(yellow) means "four," etc.]

THE SPIRIT OF THE HEARTH.

In the days of the Ming dynasty (1368-
1628 A. D.) during the years called Kia-
Tsing (1522-1567 A. D.) there lived in the
province of Kiang - Shih a man named Yu

Kong. His posthumous name was Tu, and
his honorary title Liang-Chin. He was gifted
with unusual capacity and had acquired a schol-
arship as thorough as it was varied. At the
age of sixteen he received the Bachelor's degree, and had always been first in all examinations. But when he had reached the age of
thirty, he found himself in such straits that
he was obliged to give lessons for a livelihood.
He joined several Bachelors who had studied
at the same college and commenced with them
to offer sacrifices to Wen-Chang Ti Chün, the
"Lord Superior of Scripture Glory." He carefully guarded written paper,* and set at liberty captive birds; he refrained from enjoying
the pleasures of sense, from the killing of animals, and from the sins of the tongue. Although he had faithfully observed these rules
of conduct for many years, he failed seven
times in competitive examination for the second degree.

He married and had five sons; the fourth

---

* According to Chinese views it is impious to throw
away paper on which characters are inscribed, because words,
both printed or written, are deemed to partake of the spiritual
nature of the Tao; and this notion is not altogether foreign to
the Western idea that the Logos or "word" is the incarnation
of God. There is a class of Taoist monks who devote themselves to the task of collecting and burning all scraps of inscribed paper to spare their writing the sorry fate of defile-
ment.

fell ill and died a premature death. His third
son, a child of rare intelligence and charming
features, had two black spots under the sole
of his left foot. He was an especial favorite
with his parents, but one day when he was
eight years old, while playing in the street he
lost his way and no one knew what had become of him. Yu Kong had four daughters,
but only one lived, and his wife lost her sight
from mourning for her childern. Although
he worked incessantly year after year, his misery only increased from day to day. So he
examined himself, and finding he had committed no great sin, became resigned, although
not without murmuring, to heaven's chasten-
ing hand.

When he had passed the age of forty, every
year at the end of the twelfth moon he wrote
a prayer on yellow paper and burned it before
the Spirit of the Hearth, beseeching him to
carry his vows to heaven. This practice he
continued for several years without having
the slightest response.

When he was forty-seven, he spent the last
evening of the year in the company of his blind
wife and only daughter. Gathered together
in a room very scantily furnished, the three
tried to console one another in their afflictions,
when all at once a knock was heard at the

door. Yu Kong took the lamp and went to
see who it was, and lo, there stood a man whose
beard and hair were partly whitened by age.
The stranger was clad in black and wore a
square cap. He entered with a bow and sat
down. "My family name is Chang," he said
to Yu Kong, "I have come hither a long distance because I have heard your sighs and com-
plaints, and wish to comfort you in your distress."

Yu Kong was filled with wonder and paid
him every mark of respectful deference. "All
my life," he said to Chang, "I have conse-
crated to study and the pursuit of virtue, and
yet up to this day have never been able to obtain any advancement. Death has robbed me
of nearly all my children, my wife has lost her
sight, and we can hardly earn enough to keep
us from hunger and cold. Moreover," he
added, "I have never ceased importuning the
Spirit of the Hearth and burning before him
written prayers."

"For many years," Chang replied, "I have
taken an interest in the affairs of your house,
and I am sorry that with your evil thoughts
you have filled the measure to overflowing.
Concerned only to acquire empty renown you
sent to heaven unacceptable prayers, filled with

murmurings and accusations. I fear that your
visitation is not yet at an end."

Yu Kong was frightened. "I have heard,"
he said with emotion, "that in the other world
even the smallest virtues are written in a book.
I have sworn to do good, and for a long time
have carefully followed the rules which are
laid down for men. Can you then say that I
have worked for mere vainglory?"

"My friend," Chang answered, "among
those precepts there is one which bids you to
respect written characters. Yet your pupils
and fellow students often use the leaves of ancient books to redress the walls of their rooms
and to make enveloxes; some, indeed, even use
them to wipe off their tables. Then they ex-
cuse themselves by saying that although they
soil the paper, they burn it immediately afterwards. This happens daily under your eyes
and you say not a word to prevent it. Indeed
when you yourself find a scrap of written paper in the street you take it home and throw it
in the fire. While you suffer others to trespass,
tell me please what good does it do that you
act rightly? It is true, too, that every month
you set animals at liberty that have been
doomed to death; but in this you blindly follow
the crowd and act only according to the coun-
sel of others. It would even seem that you re-

main undecided and irresolute if others do not
first set the example. Good feeling and com-
passion have never been spontaneous in your
heart. You have kids and lobsters served on
your table, without considering that they, too,
are endowed with the breath of life. As to
the sins of the tongue, you shine by reason of
your readiness of speech and force of argument
and never fail to silence all who dispute with
you, but you are insentient to the fact that
thereby you wound others' feelings and lose
their friendship. Often, too, carried away by
the heat of discussion, you take advantage of
your superiority and taunt your opponents
with biting sarcasm. You pierce them with
the bitter darts of your tongue and thus draw
upon you the anger of the gods. You are una-
ware of the number of your offences which are
recorded in the spiritual world, and yet you
picture yourself the most virtuous of men. Who
is there who pretends to deceive me? Do you
think any one can impose upon heaven?

"It is true that you commit no actual
crimes; but when you meet a beautiful woman
in another's home and cannot banish her from
your thoughts, you have committed adultery
with her in your heart. Consider a moment!
Would you have sufficient control over yourself to imitate the sage Lu Nan-Tze if you

were placed in a similar position? When he once found himself obliged to pass the night in a house whose only other occupant was a woman, he lighted a lamp and read aloud until morning to avoid exposing her to unjust suspicions.* You say that you have kept yourself pure and unspotted throughout your life, and believe that you can without fear present yourself before heaven and earth, before demons and spirits! You are deceiving yourself. If this is the way you have followed the precepts which you have sworn to observe, what need is there to speak of others?

"I have presented to heaven the supplications which you have burned before my altar. The Supreme Master has charged a spirit to keep careful account of your good and evil deeds, and for several years he has not found a single virtue worth recording. When you are alone and given over to yourself, I see nothing in your heart but thoughts of avarice, of envy, of selfishness; thoughts of pride, of scorn and of ambition; and thoughts of hate and ingratitude towards your benefactors and your friends. These thoughts grow on you;

---

* See Mayers, *Chinese Reader's Manual,* Nos. 429 and 403. This incident is commonly told of Kwang Yü, deified as Kwang Ti, the Chinese god of war. Cf. *ibid.,* No. 297, where the common version of Lu Nan-Tze's adventure as told by Mayers, differs somewhat from our story.

so plentifully they swarm in the depths of your heart that I could not enumerate them all. The gods have already recorded a vast number of them and the punishment of heaven is increasing daily. Since you have not even time to escape the calamities which threaten you, what use to pray for happiness!"

At these words Yu Kong was panic-stricken. He prostrated himself upon the earth and burst into a torrent of tears.

"Oh Lord!" he groaned, "I know that thou art a god since thou knowest things which are hidden. Have mercy upon me and save me!"

"My friend," Chang replied, "you study the works of the ancients, you are instructed in your duties, and love of truth has always been a delight to you. When you hear a noble word, you are for the moment carried away with zeal and emulation, while if you witness a good action, your heart leaps for very joy. But as soon as these things are out of your sight and hearing, you forget them at once. Faith has not planted her roots deeply in your heart, and therefore your good principles have no solid foundation. Then, too, the good words and actions of your whole life have never been anything but empty show. Have you ever done a single thing that betrayed a noble motive? And yet, when your heart is full of wrong thoughts which surround and bind you on all sides, you dare ask heaven for the rewards which only virtue can claim. You are like a man who would sow only thistles and thorns in his field and expect a rich harvest of good fruit. Would not that be the height of folly?

"From this time forward, arm yourself with courage, and banish all impure and unworthy thoughts that may present themselves to your mind. You must first bring forth a crop of pure and noble thoughts, and after that you may direct your efforts to the accomplishment of good. If an opportunity comes to do a good action which is within the limits of your strength, hasten to do it with a firm and resolute heart, without calculating whether it is large or small, difficult or easy, or whether it will bring you any advantage. If this good act is above your strength, use the same zeal and effort in order to show your sincere intention. Your first duty is patience without limit, your second, tireless perseverance. Above all, keep yourself from indifference and avoid self-deception. When you have followed these rules of conduct for a long time you will reap untold benefits.

"Within your home you have served me with a pure and reverential heart and it is for this reason that I have come with the especial purpose of bringing you instructions. If you make haste to carry them out with all your might you may appease heaven and cause it to change its decision."

While speaking the stranger entered farther within the house. Yu Kong rose eagerly and followed. But on approaching the hearth, the weird visitor vanished. Then Yu Kong realized that it was the Spirit of the Hearth who presides over the destiny of men. He at once burned incense in his honor and prostrated himself in grateful acknowledgment.

The next day which was the first day of the first month of the year, he directed prayers and praise to heaven. He avoided his former errors and began to do well with a sincere heart. He changed his literary name to Tseng-I Tao-Jen which means "the Taoist bent on the purification of his heart," and then wrote out a vow to banish all blameworthy thoughts.

The first day he was besieged by a thousand conflicting thoughts; now he fell into doubt, and again into indifference and inaction. He allowed hours and days to pass fruitlessly and it was not long before he returned to the path in which he had before lost his way. At last he prostrated himself before the altar of

the great Kwan Yin* whom he worshiped in
his home, and shed tears of blood.

"I vow," he said, "that my only desire is
to have none but worthy thoughts, to keep
myself pure and unspotted, and to use every
effort to advance towards perfection. If I
relax a hair's breadth may I fall into the depths
of hell."

Every day he rose very early and invoked
one hundred times in sincerity and faith the
holy name of Ta-Tzé Ta-Peï (the Most Benevolent and Most Compassionate One) that
he might obtain divine aid. From that moment
he controlled his thoughts, words, and actions
as if spirits were constantly at his side. He
dared not permit himself the slightest waver-
ing.

Whenever anything occurred to him that
might be of use to man or beast, he did not

---

*Kwan Yin, or in full Kwan-Shih-Yin Tze-Tsai, is the
Buddha of mercy, a divinity which is peculiarly Chinese, hav-
ing incorporated features of the founder of Buddhism but
being represented as a goddess. She is the most popular
deity in China and is in many respects comparable to the
Virgin Mary in Roman Catholic countries. Her name in
Tibet is Tara; her Chinese name is an abbreviation of the
Sanskrit *Avalokitesvara* which means the *Isvara,* or sovereign
Lord, and *avaloki,* on-looking, i. e., considerate.

In the *Saddharma-pundarika,* Chapter XXIV, (*S. B. E.,*
XXI, p. 410 *et seq.*), she is referred to as a preacher of the
Good Law, and this chapter is recited daily both morning and
evening in Buddhist temples.

consider whether it was a great or a small
thing, whether he had time or was too busily
engaged, or whether he had or had not sufficient ability and means to perform it. He
hastened to undertake it with enthusiasm, and
stopped only after its complete accomplishment. He did good as often as he found opportunity and spread benefits in secret far and
wide. He performed every duty faithfully and
applied himself to study untiringly. He practiced humility, bore insults, and endeavored to
influence to well-doing all the men that he met.
The days were not long enough for his good
works. On the last day of each month he made
a list on yellow paper of all his acts and words
during the thirty preceding days and burned
it before the Spirit of the Hearth.

Yu Kong soon ripened in the practice of
noble deeds. While he was up and doing every
one of his acts was followed by a thousand
good results, and when he rested no blameworthy thought troubled the serenity of his
soul. So he continued for three years.

When Yu Kong reached the age of fifty,
in the second year of the reign of Wan Li
(1574 A. D.), Chang Kiang-Lin who held the
office of First Minister of State, sought an in-
structor for his son, and with one voice, every
one recommended Yu Kong for the place. The

Minister himself went to invite him, and brought him and his family to the capital.

Chang, who appreciated Yu Kong's strength of character, induced him to enter the imperial college, and in the year Ping-Tsée (1576 A. D.) he competed for and obtained the degree of Licentiate and the next year was raised to the rank of Tsin-Ssé (Doctor).

One day while still sojourning in the capital, he went to visit a eunuch whose name was Yang Kong. Yang introduced his five adopted sons whom he had purchased in different parts of the realm to be a comfort to him in his old age; and there was among them a youth of sixteen years, whose face seemed somehow familiar to Yu Kong. So he asked him where he was born.

"I am from the district of Kiang-Shih," the youth replied. "When I was a child I became lost by heedlessly embarking with a cargo of grain. The name of my family and also my native village are very dim in my memory."

Yu Kong was surprised and deeply moved. Begging the youth to uncover his left foot he recognized the two black spots and cried out, "You are my son!"

Yang Kong rejoiced at the good fortune of this happy meeting and allowed the father to take his son home. The blind mother embraced her son tenderly and shed tears of sorrow and joy. The boy wept too and pressing his mother's face between his hands, gently touched her eyes with his tongue and instantly she recovered her sight.* Yu Kong's happiness was now complete, and in spite of the tears with which his eyes were still moist, his face beamed with joy.

From this time Yu Kong gave up his situation and took leave of Chan Kiang-Lin to return to his native village. The Minister, however, affected by the nobility of his tutor's character, would not permit him to leave until he had presented him with many rich gifts.

Having reached his native country, Yu Kong continued his good deeds with increased zeal. His son married, and had in his turn, seven sons, all of whom lived to inherit the talents and renown of their grandfather.

Yu Kong wrote a book in which he told the history of his life before and after his happy conversion, and gave the book to his grandsons to learn from his experiences. He lived to the age of eighty-eight years, and every one looked upon his long life as the just reward for his

* According to a very ancient belief spittle is possessed of magic power. We read in the Gospel that Jesus used it for healing both the deaf (Mark vii. 33) and the blind (John ix. 6).

noble deeds by which he had changed the decision of heaven in his favor.

THE STORM DRAGON.

Shen of Tai-Ts'ang was wealthy, but a brutal and inhumane man who treated his fellow-citizens shamefully, and especially exhibited his bad character in damaging their instruments and machines, or any utensils which were used by workers in tilling the soil, manufacturing, fishing, hunting, and other occupations of life.

Once when he was building a guest hall in his house, he hired Liu of a neighboring village, well known as a skilled sculptor, to carve some figures on pillars and beams; but when the artist had finished his work Shen refused to pay him the stipulated sum. The sculptor remonstrated and the dispute was finally settled by a lawsuit against Shen, who for this reason began to scheme for revenge.

Some time later, the Buddhist priests in a southern metropolis intended to have the statues of five hundred Arhats carved for their temple, and having heard of Liu's fame, invited him to compete for the task. Shen thought his opportunity had come. So he hired a man to join Liu's party. While on the way, this villain,

THE STORM DRAGON.

following the instructions of Shen, spoiled the
instruments of the sculptor and absconded
without being discovered. When Liu on his
arrival could use none of his tools he was un-
able to compete with the native sculptors,
whereby he lost his employment and became
quite destitute.

Since Shen continued in his evil practices,
his daughter-in-law warned him that unless
he reformed, heaven would certainly visit the
family with misfortune; but Shen resented her
words and drove her from his home charging
her with impudence, and disobedience. Before
she was more than a mile or so away from
the house, there came a sudden terrific outburst
of thunder and lightning, and she hid herself
in the woods near by. Then she saw a scarlet
dragon come out of the black clouds and enter
Shen's residence. The building was completely
wrecked, everything inside destroyed and every
living thing instantly killed. No member of
the family escaped, except the daughter-in-law
who had been driven out. Heaven favored her
and she lived a long and prosperous life.

[Our illustration exhibits the typical Chinese conception of thunder and lightning. The thunder demon
holds a mallet in either hand and is surrounded by
a circle of drums and flames. Lightning is represented
as a woman from whose hands flow streams of flame.

The scarlet dragon is the storm sweeping over the country leaving destruction in its wake.]

THE ANTS.

Ho Kwan of Kuang Nan was a kind-hearted man and never killed any living thing. He had a jar containing one thousand pieces of silver which he kept in a casket. The white ants, of which there were so many in his district, invaded the casket and ate part of the silver. When his family found what had happened, they traced the ants to a hollow cave where millions of them were living. They thought if they put all of these ants in a crucible, perhaps they could recover a part of the lost silver. But Ho objected to the scheme, saying: "I cannot bear to see all these many creatures killed on account of a small sum of silver."

So they let the matter drop. That night he dreamed that scores of soldiers in white armor came to him, asking him to enter a carriage which they had with them and to come to the palace of their king. Ho Kwan proceeded with the soldiers to a town where the people looked prosperous and the buildings were all magnificent. Numerous officers came to meet him and took him to a splendid palace.

THE ANTS.

The king, clad in royal fashion, descended from the throne, and, cordially saluting Ho Kwan, said: "By your benevolent acts we have been saved from our enemy. While not forgetting your kindness, the lack of strict discipline among my people caused you some trouble recently, but by your mercy they have again been saved from calamity. How could I let your kindness go unrequited this time? There is a certain tree near your residence readily identified, under which in olden times a certain person buried a jar full of silver. Just dig that out and keep it for yourself. You are the unicorn of mankind (the emblem of perfect goodness) that will never hurt any living soul. It is a pity that you are now too old to enjoy the fruits of your kindness yourself, but your descendents will reap what you have sown."

After this Ho Kwan was escorted back to his own house as before, by armed soldiers. When he awoke he meditated on the dream and found it to be the work of the ants. So he dug up the place as told by their king and recovered a jar buried therein these many years. His son became an eminent scholar.

[Our picture is an instance of the method used by Chinese artists to represent dreams. The spirit of the sleeper is supposed to go out into the distance.

Sometimes we find the dreamer pictured in a sleeping posture with the dream curves which envelope the vision proceeding from his head.]

THE CRUEL HUNTERS.

In the county of Hsiang-Tan in Hu-Kuang there was an old and much respected gentleman. He had three sons who did not care for culture and refinement but spent every day in sports and roaming through the mountains.

One day the three went out hunting with a large company of young people and they met unexpectedly an old man in white garments who knelt and thus addressed them: "To refrain from injuring all growing things and from killing whatever is awakening into life is the part of universal lovingkindness as observed by saints and sages. It is now springtime when everything in nature is starting to life again. If you pay no attention to the tenderness of heart as practiced by holy men, and by unchecking the wild passions lurking in men's hearts, if you set the woods afire and exterminate the animals and insects that inhabit them, you will surely incur heavenly displeasure and suffer the consequences thereof. I, poor old creature, have seven young children in my family, and there is not time to remove

THE CRUEL HUNTERS.

them to a place of safety; but if you, gentlemen, have pity on us, we will never forget your mercy and will reward you later."

The three leaders of the party did not exactly understand what the old man wanted but without further thought promised to do as he had requested.

When the old man was gone some of the party began to wonder who he could have been and whence he might have come into this wilderness; and they argued that his appeal to their sympathy did not sound human. Possibly he was the spirit of some old wild animal living around in the mountains.

Upon this suggestion they pursued him, and seeing him enter a cave, spread a net before it and started a fire in the entrance. Suddenly a white stag darted forth from the hole, and breaking through the besiegers, climbed up to a near rock, and then assuming the form of an old man, turned back to the hunting party, exclaiming: "You have killed my seven young daughters. You shall have to pay a penalty for this heartless act. A calamity ten times greater than I have suffered, will befall your family."

The three young men tried to shoot him, but he caught up the arrows in his hands and breaking them to pieces disappeared.

Later, there came to their house a Taoist monk who predicted for them an imperial career and great prosperity for the future. Incited by this prophecy, they organized a rebellion in which many of their friends joined, for the purpose of overthrowing the reigning dynasty and establishing a new government under their own leadership. While the preparations were going on secretly, somebody betrayed their conspiracy to the authorities. Soldiers were immediately dispatched to their home, and, surrounding the house, put every one of the family under arrest. On examination they were found guilty of treason. Seventy members of their families and associates were executed according to law; but nobody ever knew what became of the Taoist monk who had been the real leader of the scheme. He as well as the man who had betrayed them disappeared.

[This curious story, especiallly the figure of the mountain spirit who acts as a protector of wild animals, reminds us of Schiller's poem, *Der Alpenjäger*, which we quote entire from Bulwer-Lytton's translation, slightly modified:

THE ALPINE HUNTER.

" 'Wilt thou not be lambkins heeding?
Innocent and gentle, they
Meekly on sweet herbs are feeding,

And beside the brook they play.'
'Mother, keep me not at home,
Let me as a hunter roam!'

' 'Wilt thou not, thy herds assembling,
Lure with lively horn along?—
Sweet their clear bells tinkle trembling,
Sweet the echoing woods among!'
'Mother, mother, let me go,
O'er the wilds to chase the roe.'

" 'Wilt thou nurture not the flowers,
Tend them like my own dear child?
Dark and drear the mountain lowers,
Wild is nature on the wild!'
'Leave the flowers in peace to blow.
Mother, mother, let me go!'

"Forth the hunter bounds unheeding,
On his hardy footsteps press;
Hot and eager, blindly speeding
To the mountain's last recess.
Swift before him, as the wind,
Panting trembling, flies the hind.

"Up the ribbed crag-tops driven,
Up she clambers, steep on steep;
O'er the rocks asunder riven
Springs her dizzy, daring leap:
Still unwearied, with the bow
Of death, behind her flies the foe.

"On the peak that rudely, drearly
Jags the summit, bleak and hoar,
Where the rocks, descending sheerly,

Leave to flight no path before;
There she halts at last, to find
Chasms beneath—the foe behind!

"To the hard man—dumb-lamenting,
Turns her look of pleading woe;
Turns in vain—the Unrelenting
Meets the look—and bends the bow,—
Yawn'd the rock; from his abode
Th' Ancient of the mountain strode;

"And his godlike hand extending,
To protect her from her foe,
'Wherefore death and slaughter sending,
Bringst thou to my realm this woe?
Shall my herds before thee fall?
Room there is on earth for all!' "]

A CHINESE HOME MISSION PUBLISHING COMPANY.

There are Bible societies in Europe and America, the contributors to which deem it meritorious to publish and propagate the canonical books of Christianity; and in China we meet with analogous sentiments which prompt people to spread abroad religious books proclaiming the moral principles of their faith. The Chinese think to gain merit by writing, copying, or publishing such books as the *Kan Ying P'ien,* and our illustration represents a publishing office maintained either by some

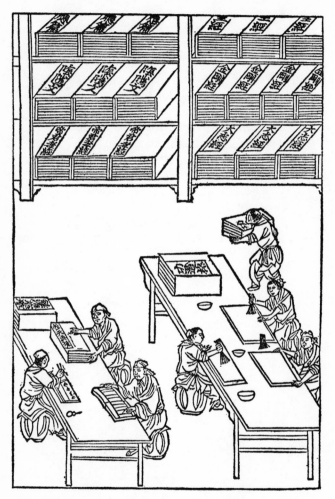

A CHINESE HOME MISSION PUBLISHING COMPANY.

pious man who is possessed of sufficient wealth,
or an association inspired by the same motive.
It is the picture of a Chinese Home Mission
Publishing Company.

We see in the lower left-hand corner two
engravers busily employed in writing characters upon engraving blocks. At the further
end of the table stands a pile of tracts, *Yü
Hai Tze Hang,* which treat of the "Voyage of
Mercy over the Ocean of Desire," a Buddhist
Pilgrim's Progress. A man is engaged in stor-
ing away another tract, the *Hsing T'ien Yüh
Ching,* which discusses the subject "how with
a heavenly nature we may adjust ourselves to
circumstances."

At the right-hand table where the three
men are printing with brushes, we see another
tract, the *Kung Kuo Ko,* which means "the
Table of Merits and Demerits" — a curious
little book which is incorporated as an appen-
dix to the Chinese copy of the *Kan Ying P'ien*
in our possession. It contains a list of all good
and evil deeds, and marks their value in figures
in a system similar to that in use in our schools.
Stopping a fight counts $+3$; inducing people
to abstain from eating flesh for one year counts
$+20$; gossiping with evil tongue, -3; to return favors, $+20$; to keep a promise seems to

be considered as a matter of course, for it counts but +1; to abstain from taking things that do not belong to us, counts also but +1; sincerity, or, as the book expresses it, "to speak as one thinks,"counts +1 per day; betrayal of a neighbor's secrets counts —50. At the end of the book there are blanks for lists of both meritorious and demeritorious deeds, for the sums total on both sides, and for the statement of the balance.

The pile of tracts which is just being carried to the shelves is a volume of the same book, as may be recognized by the first word *kung,* "merits."

The stacks in the background contain the following books: on the left upper shelf are three rows of the *Kan-Ying P'ien;* on the left middle shelf is the *Yin Chih Wên,* or *The Tract of the Quiet Way;** on the left lower shelf we read the title *Ti Chün Hsiao King,* "The Imperial Lord's Book of Filial Piety," a work of Taoist ethics, probably written in the same strain as the *Kan-Ying P'ien;* on the right upper shelf is the "Canonical Book (*King*) of the Pearly Emperor"; on the right middle shelf we see a Buddhist book called "The Diamond Cutter," *Chin Kang King,* a

* Chicago: The Open Court Publishing Co., 1906.

well-known treatise published in English translation among the *Sacred Books of the East;* and on the lowest right-hand shelf is to be found the *Ta Chih King,* or "Book of Great Thoughts."

INDEX.